Overview

Introduction

For years, I desired to spend time alone with God. Or, maybe more accurately, I knew I should spend time alone with God, but I couldn't seem to find something that would stick. I couldn't seem to find something I'd want to do consistently. Now, after having developed the rhythm of meeting with God every day and experiencing all the incredible gifts God has for me every morning, I realize how much I suffered from a lack of direct connection with my heavenly Father when I went even one day without spending time alone with him.

My awakening happened during the last campus worship service in the fall of my sophomore year at college. I was spiritually and physically exhausted. I had this hole in my heart that needed to be filled—a void longing for affirmation, for love. Because I had never discovered how to fill that hole with the unconditional love of the Father, I was working every day to be affirmed and loved by man, a love wrought with conditions, a love I could never count on.

I was at the end of myself. Sitting on the front pew of Second Baptist Church of Arkadelphia, Arkansas, I prayed one of the first honest prayers of my life. It wasn't eloquent. But it was real. I said, "God, I don't know what to do, but I know you do. Tell me what to do, and I'll do it." I reached my hand out to a God I knew was real but a God I didn't know how to have real relationship with. At that moment, I heard the voice of my Father speak to me. It wasn't audible, but it was as clear and real as day.

He said, "It just needs to be me and you for a while."

I knew exactly what God meant. With his words was a very present, unmistakable meaning: *Stop seeking love from others and start seeking it in me. Stop looking for value and identity out in the world and start discovering your value and identity as my beloved.* He directed my eyes away from the external and drew my gaze inward, to his Spirit fellowshiping with my spirit. That moment was a catalyst for a journey that changed my life—a journey of learning how to spend time alone with my Father.

Wherever you are on your journey, I hope this book helps you discover new depths of conscious communion with a God who loves you more than you could ever know. You were made to spend time alone with God. You were made to dwell in his presence, hear his voice, and know his love in a way that roots you and establishes you in God's life-changing goodness. His love will shelter you from the fickle opinion of others around you. His love will satisfy your heart in a way that equips you to live a full, inwardly abundant life. His love will empower you to abide in him that you might bear real, eternal fruit in this life.

If it's been difficult for you to establish consistency in spending time alone with God, or if you've been spending time with him for years, God has amazing things in store for you as you make space to meet with him. My prayer is that this book will serve as a catalyst for you to experience greater depths of God's presence as you discover how available he truly is. May you find the courage to be more honest and vulnerable in the grace of the Father. May you learn powerful and practical truths that equip you to open your hands a little more to receive all the amazing gifts God has for you as you grow in unveiled relationship with him.

May your heart come alive as you seek him who loved you first.

A Guide to *Catalyst*

Establishing and maximizing my rhythm of spending time alone with God every day meant discovering real answers to some big questions I had.

WHY SHOULD I SPEND TIME ALONE WITH GOD?

I can't do something for very many days, especially something that isn't mandatory, unless I know why it's good for me. Until the *should* becomes a *want,* I will never be consistent.

HOW DO I SPEND TIME ALONE WITH GOD?

One of my biggest barriers to spending time alone with God was figuring out what to do with the time I set aside. I know I should read the Bible, but what part should I read and for how long? I know I should pray, but doesn't God know everything I need and everything that's bothering me anyway? And I've never been one to keep a diary, so what's a journal for? I found that unless I woke up with these questions answered, I felt automatically drawn to something with clearer benefits, like entertainment or work.

HOW DO I GET THE MOST OUT OF MY TIME ALONE WITH GOD?

One of the reasons I quit spending time alone with God so quickly after starting is that I didn't know how to maximize the time. As soon as I got bored—and checking a box wasn't enough of a driver for me—I would quit. Learning core truths about the amazing, life-changing gifts God had for me each day changed everything for me. It shifted time alone with God from a *should* to my favorite time of the day.

LASTLY, HOW DO I BUILD A SOLID FOUNDATION OF SPENDING TIME ALONE WITH GOD?

At different points in my journey of establishing a life-giving time alone with God, I discovered truths that became cornerstones for me, truths I wished someone had shared with me from the start. Doing anything every day is difficult, let alone spending time alone with a God without physical form and whom most every human ignores. So, core truths about who God is and what he has for us as we meet with him are vital in swimming upstream every day and choosing God's kingdom over the world.

Every week of this 28-day devotional handles one of these questions. Every day we'll either explore a principle that will deepen your experience or discover one practical truth that will strengthen your ability to seek God no matter what life brings your way.

The best thing you could do to receive all that God intends for you through this book is to begin with a mindset of grace rather than works. This is not another book intended to create another box you need to check. You already have more people telling you things you should do than you can handle, and the last thing I want to be is yet another voice telling you you're not enough.

The point is not failure or success, finished or unfinished. The point is that you would grow in your relationship with God. All God cares about is that you would have his heart and he would have yours. So, engage with this book with that end in mind and that end only. God's goodness and love are more than enough to draw you into a rhythm of meeting with him every day. There's no room for obligation or guilt in a relationship with a God who holds in his hands everything you need, everything you were created for.

As we embark on this journey of going deeper into the immeasurable, limitless kindness of our heavenly Father, may your heart be richly satisfied and life made better by making time for the most important and life-giving relationship you'll ever have: your relationship with God.

WEEK

Why?

ONE

The Power of Why

WEEKLY OVERVIEW

In our first week of *Catalyst*, we'll explore seven answers to the heart's most important question: "Why?" Until we understand why spending time alone with God every day is worth the time and energy it takes, we'll never be able to develop consistency or go as deep into God's presence as we were created for. May you realize both the depth of your need and the goodness and availability of your Father as you discover your *why*.

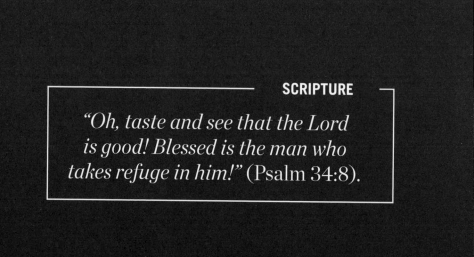

SCRIPTURE

"Oh, taste and see that the Lord is good! Blessed is the man who takes refuge in him!" (Psalm 34:8).

I wish I were one of those people who would do things just because I should. I wish that my discipline were greater than my desires. But I've grown to accept the simple truth: it just isn't. The only things I do consistently, I do because I want to. And I'm learning that that's kind of OK. In fact, I'm learning that God's intention is for my heart to align with his—that I would live as an authentic disciple of Jesus out of love for him, not obligation. I'm learning the key that unlocks authentic desire to meet with my heavenly Father is discovering the answer to a powerful, one-word question: "Why?"

> *The only things I do consistently, I do because I want to.*

I spent years feeling bad for even asking the question. I ignored the question, tried to get past it, and tried to live as if I knew how badly I needed time alone with the Father. But the truth is that if I really believed I needed it, if I really understood why spending time one-on-one with God was so important, I would have been doing it.

Looking back, I see two issues were at play in my heart. I hated how I felt when I realized that I didn't value spending time alone with God as much as the other things I was spending my time on. And I didn't believe that there was a good enough answer to my question of why, and that scared me.

I mean, what if spending time alone with God really is boring? What if the Bible doesn't really apply much to my life? What if I never like worship songs as much as other music? What then?

Rather than bringing the question before God in faith that he truly was good enough to have a life-changing answer, I shoved the question down time and time again. It wasn't until I got so desperate for something more, so desperate for a different way of living, that I came to God with my question of why and discovered answers that changed everything for me. It wasn't until my desperation gave me the courage to be honest before God that I discovered that he was actually thrilled to explore my question together.

Before we explore some powerful reasons for why spending time alone with God really is worth our time and energy, let's take time to bring our question of why before our good and wise Father. Let's take time to *"taste and see that the Lord is good"* (Psalm 34:8). Let's allow the Holy Spirit to fill our hearts with the courage to be honest about those things that are holding us back from diving heart first into greater depths of our relationship with him. May we discover a God who is better and wiser than we thought—a God both more aware of our questions than we knew and more thrilled to address those questions than we could have imagined.

May God illuminate any why within your heart and give you a sense of his grace and love as you enter a time of guided prayer today.

Notes:

GUIDED PRAYER

1. Take a moment to be still and receive God's presence. Reflect on the facts that God is already all around you and he has promised his presence to you. Ask the Holy Spirit to reveal his nearness in a real, tangible way.

   "Where shall I go from your Spirit? Or where shall I flee from your presence? If I ascend to heaven, you are there! If I make my bed in Sheol, you are there! If I take the wings of the morning and dwell in the uttermost parts of the sea, even there your hand shall lead me, and your right hand shall hold me.' If I say, 'Surely the darkness shall cover me, and the light about me be night,' even the darkness is not dark to you; the night is bright as the day, for darkness is as light with you" (Psalm 139:7–12).

2. Where do you feel prone to give yourself more to the world or others than to God? What often takes the place of spending time alone with God or distracts you from going deeper in your time alone with him? Know that God isn't angry with you. He's actually thrilled to give you wisdom and revelation. Journal what thoughts come to mind to help you focus.

   "If any of you lacks wisdom, let him ask God, who gives generously to all without reproach, and it will be given him" (James 1:5).

3. Ask God for one answer to why spending time alone with him is worth what it costs you. Ask him for a gift he wants to give you, like freedom, peace, or revelation. Ask him why he wants to meet with you, specifically you. Take a moment to be silent and create space for him to speak. Pay attention to any way you sense him answering you.

GO . . .

Take notice of how you spend your time today. What matters most to you that you would give it your most valuable possessions: your time and attention? God looks at you with total grace. He isn't mad. He's happy that you even want to meet with him, to go deeper with him. He's so good that he takes whatever you offer and multiplies its impact like Jesus did with the bread and fish.

Taking an inventory of your time allows you to be more intentional and make space for that which matters most: your relationship with God. The path to intentional living, of aligning your time and attention with God's *why*, takes time and is never really finished. But it's a path that leads to greater and greater depths of abundant life.

May you grow in your desire to abide in God today as you take inventory of the people and pursuits that matter most to you. Sense God's profound grace and love for you throughout your day.

God's Heart to Meet with You

WEEKLY OVERVIEW

In our first week of *Catalyst*, we'll explore seven answers to the heart's most important question: "Why?" Until we understand why spending time alone with God every day is worth the time and energy it takes, we'll never be able to develop consistency or go as deep into God's presence as we were created for. May you realize both the depth of your need and the goodness and availability of your Father as you discover your *why*.

SCRIPTURE

"How precious to me are your thoughts, O God! How vast is the sum of them! If I would count them, they are more than the sand. I awake, and I am still with you" (Psalm 139:17–18).

DEVOTIONAL

The most life-changing moment I've had with God apart from my salvation was discovering that he really wants to meet with me—not just people in general, but me specifically. God sees me as I am. He knows all of my past sins and present failures. And yet, he genuinely wants to spend time with me.

We serve a God who constantly, sweetly, and powerfully pursues us. Revelation 3:20 says, *"Behold, I stand at the door and knock. If anyone hears my voice and opens the door, I will come in to him and eat with him, and he with me."* God is knocking on the door of your heart right now. He is not distant. His focus isn't elsewhere. He's focused on you, and his heart is filled with the desire to love you, lead you, and fill you with his Spirit.

The first and most foundational answer to the question of why we should spend time alone with God every day is that we were created to live with a constant awareness of God's unconditional love. The foundation of our why will always be God's why. God's greatest desire is for a restored relationship with his people. And it's in knowing and receiving his unceasing desire for us that our hearts will be stirred to meet with him.

> *You weren't made to live apart from the love and approval of your heavenly Father.*

A relationship with God is incredibly similar to relationships with others. We're naturally drawn to people who care for us. We like spending time with people who enjoy spending time with us. So, discovering God's desire to meet with us is foundational to establishing the rhythm of consistently spending time alone with him.

The Creator of the universe deeply longs to continually, consistently meet with you. God, who is almighty, all-knowing, filled with grace, and is the fulfillment of perfect love, longs to be known by you. You were made to know and be known by your heavenly Father. You were created to walk with him every moment of every day. To try and live without a continual experience of God's love and desire for you is to live without nourishment for your soul, and it only leads to striving, dissatisfaction, and emptiness.

You weren't made to live apart from the love and approval of your heavenly Father. You weren't made to walk through life alone. God's intention in creating you was to dwell with you, walk with you, lead you, love you, and provide for you. Until your life aligns with God's intentions in creating you, you'll never find the sense of fulfillment and core purpose you've been looking for.

Song of Solomon 7:10 says, *"I am my beloved's, and his desire is for me."* May you grow in the awareness of God's desire for you today. May you come to know yourself as God's *"beloved."* May your life be marked by the natural response to your Creator's unending pursuit of you. And may you center your life around meeting with God, not out of obligation, but because he so lovingly longs to meet with you.

Notes:

GUIDED PRAYER

1. Meditate on God's desire to meet with you. Take in the reality that your Creator cares deeply about you and is focused on you right now.

   "Behold, I stand at the door and knock. If anyone hears my voice and opens the door, I will come in to him and eat with him, and he with me" (Revelation 3:20).

   "You did not choose me, but I chose you" (John 15:16).

2. What does it mean for your life that your loving Creator continually pursues you? What would it be like to live a life marked by responding to God's love in every moment? Journal your thoughts.

3. Take time to meet with God. Ask him how he feels about you. Ask him to reveal his desire for you. Respond to his affections with your own. Tell him how his love and pursuit of you makes you feel.

   "I am my beloved's, and his desire is for me" (Song of Solomon 7:10).

   "How precious to me are your thoughts, O God! How vast is the sum of them! If I would count them, they are more than the sand. I awake, and I am still with you" (Psalm 139:17–18).

GO . . .

All you have is today. Consistently meeting with God is more about the choices you make right now than ones you make tomorrow. The way you choose to live right now will impact your days to come. Don't worry about your track record. Don't concern yourself with the idea of meeting with Jesus every day for the rest of your life. Simply choose to enjoy him today. *"Sufficient for the day is its own trouble"* (Matthew 6:34).

One Thing Only is Necessary

WEEKLY OVERVIEW

In our first week of *Catalyst*, we'll explore seven answers to the heart's most important question: "Why?" Until we understand why spending time alone with God every day is worth the time and energy it takes, we'll never be able to develop consistency or go as deep into God's presence as we were created for. May you realize both the depth of your need and the goodness and availability of your Father as you discover your *why*.

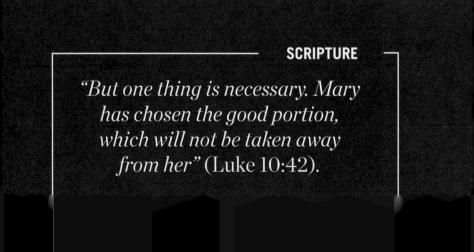

SCRIPTURE

"But one thing is necessary. Mary has chosen the good portion, which will not be taken away from her" (Luke 10:42).

"Now as they went on their way, Jesus entered a village. And a woman named Martha welcomed him into her house. And she had a sister called Mary, who sat at the Lord's feet and listened to his teaching. But Martha was distracted with much serving. And she went up to him and said, 'Lord, do you not care that my sister has left me to serve alone? Tell her then to help me.' But the Lord answered her, 'Martha, Martha, you are anxious and troubled about many things, but one thing is necessary. Mary has chosen the good portion, which will not be taken away from her.'" (Luke 10:38–42)

There is no better passage of Scripture to illustrate the biblical value of spending time alone with God than the story of Mary and Martha. Jesus' statement in verse 42 is shockingly countercultural, even to much of our Christian culture today. Jesus says that *"one thing is necessary,"* and that's to sit at his feet. The original Greek actually takes the sentiment of verse 42 even further. Jesus' statement is better translated as *"one thing only is necessary."*

> # *Jesus is calling you to a lifestyle of valuing time alone with him above all else because it's absolutely the best thing for you.*

Seeking to align my life with Luke 10:42 has changed everything for me. For most of my life, God got what was left of me, if anything at all. I viewed almost everything else in my day as necessary and time with him as ancillary—as extra. But the reality is that spending time alone with him is foundational to everything else. It's the one thing that's necessary because only from the position of sitting at Jesus' feet does every other aspect of life as God intends it find its proper place.

When I prioritize time alone with God, my family gets a husband or father able to truly love them because I've just experienced the unconditional love of Jesus, of the Father. When I work from daily being filled by the Holy Spirit, I create things from God's heart, from God's voice, and with God's leadership and anointing. When time spent alone with the Author of rest is at the center of my Sabbath, I find myself wholly revived and equipped to live with transcendent peace rather than just filling my day with entertainment.

Every word of Scripture and every statement of Jesus were written or spoken out of love for us, and Luke 10:42 is no different. God is not trying to obligate you to have time alone with him. He's not trying to add more to your plate. Rather, he wants to be the plate on which the whole of your life is made abundant, filled with the glory of his goodness.

Jesus is calling you to a lifestyle of valuing time alone with him above all else because it's absolutely the best thing for you. He knows that time alone with him is the only way you can truly abide in him and he in you. He desires to bless you beyond belief, to use you for far greater impact than you could imagine, and to make every moment richer and fuller—a true picture of what it's like to be the beloved child of a limitless, loving Father.

Take time in guided prayer now to reevaluate your priorities in light of Luke 10:42. Seek to discover what it would take for God to get the first of you rather than what's left over. And make space to experience God's goodness right now, that every moment of your day would be filled with God's abundant presence.

Notes:

GUIDED PRAYER

1. Take time to meditate on Luke 10:42. Allow the weight of Jesus' words to sink in. And commit to choosing obedience to God's word, acknowledging that every word of Scripture is fundamentally best for you.

   "One thing only is essential, and Mary has chosen it—it's the main course, and won't be taken from her" (Luke 10:42 MSG).

2. Ask the Holy Spirit to reveal one reason why spending time alone with God is necessary for you. Reflect on the parts of your life that would be better if they were built on the foundation of daily experiences with God's love.

   "So that Christ may dwell in your hearts through faith—that you, being rooted and grounded in love, may have strength to comprehend with all the saints what is the breadth and length and height and depth, and to know the love of Christ that surpasses knowledge, that you may be filled with all the fullness of God" (Ephesians 3:17–19).

3. Ask the Holy Spirit for one thing you can do to live more aligned with this value of spending time alone with God. What's one thing you could stop or start doing to make room to prioritize getting alone with God? What would it take to make space every day to sit at the feet of Jesus?

   "For this is the love of God, that we keep his commandments. And his commandments are not burdensome" (1 John 5:3).

GO . . .

God doesn't expect everything in your life to change overnight. He has grace for every day. His mercies are new every morning. Have the same grace for yourself that God does. You won't do this perfectly. But you can grow and change every day. Every day you can discover new ways to center your life around God. Rather than adopting a mindset of striving, choose to enjoy the fact that you serve a God of process. Enjoy the fact that whether you fail or succeed, God is with you through it all. And allow his grace for you and enjoyment of you to lay a foundation on which you can learn to seek him. May you be blessed as you seek to do the one thing that's necessary: to sit at the feet of your Savior, Jesus.

Jesus is the Best Thing

WEEKLY OVERVIEW

In our first week of *Catalyst*, we'll explore seven answers to the heart's most important question: "Why?" Until we understand why spending time alone with God every day is worth the time and energy it takes, we'll never be able to develop consistency or go as deep into God's presence as we were created for. May you realize both the depth of your need and the goodness and availability of your Father as you discover your *why*.

SCRIPTURE

"So we have come to know and to believe the love that God has for us. God is love, and whoever abides in love abides in God, and God abides in him" (1 John 4:16).

DEVOTIONAL

Of all the amazing gifts God gives us, boundless and unhindered relationship with Jesus vastly exceeds them all. Jesus is the best thing we will ever know. His love restores, satisfies, transforms, and heals. His grace empowers and brings transcendent peace. His nearness resolves the great fears of our hearts. And his kingship calls us to a right lifestyle of living for heaven rather than a pursuit of that which is worldly and fleeting. Colossians 3:1–4 says,

> *If then you have been raised with Christ, seek the things that are above, where Christ is, seated at the right hand of God. Set your minds on things that are above, not on things that are on earth. For you have died, and your life is hidden with Christ in God. When Christ who is your life appears, then you also will appear with him in glory.*

You and I have limited space in our hearts. Often, we're too busy filling ourselves up with the things of the world to leave space for the best thing. It's for that reason Jesus says in Matthew 6:33, *"Seek first the kingdom of God and his righteousness, and all these things will be added to you."* When we make space to be filled with the presence of God, to sit at the feet of Jesus, every other good thing God longs to give us will be added to our lives. It's the promise of an all-powerful, good God. And when we make space to *"seek the things that are above,"* we properly see and prioritize that which is below, filling our lives with purpose and clarity.

The best way to seek first the kingdom of God, the most foundational rhythm we could develop, is to set our hearts on Jesus at the start of each day. Before the world entices us, before the cares of work, life, and family have a chance to fill up the capacity of our hearts, we need to experience the love, peace, and rest that comes from sitting at the feet of our Savior.

Unless we make room for the best thing, unhindered communion with God, our hearts will become filled up with that which will never satisfy, that which will tether us to a world that is no longer our home. Every morning, we wake up to a split road. We will either choose to seek God first and walk the path of communion with the Spirit, or we'll choose the path of the world and join the masses searching for fulfillment in that which is fleeting, that which is folly. The first step we take on that road often determines the direction of our entire day.

> "Seek first the kingdom of God and his righteousness, and all these things will be added to you."

Too few choose the path God lays before them that leads to abundant life. Too few experience the fullness of joy that comes from filling up on the best thing. But you have the choice. You have the ability to experience Jesus right now. You have the choice to walk the path the Good Shepherd has laid out before you with him at your side. You have the choice every day to prioritize your relationship with God and experience the fullness of life Jesus died to give you.

Choose today to fill up on the best thing, the presence of God, and discover what it's like to live full and satisfied, experiencing a lifestyle of God adding every good thing to you as you seek him first.

Notes:

GUIDED PRAYER

1. Reflect for a moment on the split road you face each morning. Reflect on the differences between God's path and the path of the world. Come to terms with the reality of the decision that only you can make every day, and think for a moment about the rewards that lie at the end of each path.

"Do not love the world or the things in the world. If anyone loves the world, the love of the Father is not in him. For all that is in the world—the desires of the flesh and the desires of the eyes and pride of life—is not from the Father but is from the world. And the world is passing away along with its desires, but whoever does the will of God abides forever" (1 John 2:15–17).

"The Lord is my shepherd; I shall not want" (Psalm 23:1).

2. What things of the world have you been pursuing? In what ways has the world crowded out space that was meant solely for the things of God? Journal your thoughts.

3. Ask God to give you the grace to choose the best thing. Take time right now to receive the presence of Jesus. Ask Jesus to reveal his heart to you. Ask the Spirit for a vision of what he wants your day to look like as you walk the path of communion with him. Allow God to draw you toward his ways and surrender whatever hinders your journey to wholehearted devotion.

"But one thing is necessary. Mary has chosen the good portion, which will not be taken away from her" (Luke 10:42).

GO . . .

You have a very real enemy whose chief objective is to draw you away from experiencing God. He does that by tempting you to sin in efforts to separate you from God. He does that by enticing you to spend all your time on that which is good to keep you from that which is best. He knows your past. He knows your tendencies. But his pull is not stronger than the love of God. His ability to draw your sight to the world is not more powerful than God's ability to draw your eyes to heaven. Rest in the fact that God is drawing you—God is pursuing you. Recognize the schemes of the enemy in your life. And celebrate that you can choose every day to live filled with the presence of God.

Your Heart's Treasure

WEEKLY OVERVIEW

In our first week of *Catalyst*, we'll explore seven answers to the heart's most important question: "Why?" Until we understand why spending time alone with God every day is worth the time and energy it takes, we'll never be able to develop consistency or go as deep into God's presence as we were created for. May you realize both the depth of your need and the goodness and availability of your Father as you discover your *why*.

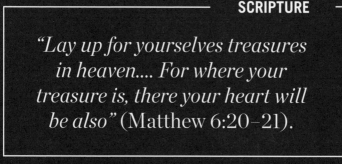

SCRIPTURE

"Lay up for yourselves treasures in heaven.... For where your treasure is, there your heart will be also" (Matthew 6:20–21).

DEVOTIONAL

In Matthew 6:19–21, Jesus teaches us another important spiritual principle we need to know to discover the value of time alone with God. Scripture says:

> *Do not lay up for yourselves treasures on earth, where moth and rust destroy and where thieves break in and steal, but lay up for yourselves treasures in heaven, where neither moth nor rust destroys and where thieves do not break in and steal. For where your treasure is, there your heart will be also.*

You are the child of a loving God who is desperately jealous for the entirety of your heart. Matthew 6:19–21 illustrates a truth that spans beyond this world and into the fullness of eternity. You and I have an opportunity in this life to either give our hearts to God and receive an eternal reward or to give our hearts to the world and accumulate rewards that pass away with us. We can either surrender all that we are and have to the perfect, pleasing plans of our heavenly Father or seek fulfillment, pleasure, status, and wealth in a life as fleeting as a breath (Psalm 144:4).

> *You and I have an opportunity in this life to either give our hearts to God and receive an eternal reward or to give our hearts to the world and accumulate rewards that pass away with us.*

You have a chance every morning to invest your heart in the kingdom of God. Each new day requires a new decision on your part. Will today be spent seeking God or seeking the world? There is no middle ground, and only one choice will produce eternal fruit. Only one choice produces eternal reward.

Only one choice will produce true satisfaction and abundant life.

God is after your heart above all else. He cares more about how you're doing than what you can do for him. He doesn't need you. He wants you. Beginning every day with the decision to give God your heart, to let him have all of you, is the path to living a life with real, eternal value. Investing your life in heaven is simple but incredibly countercultural. That's why, if you want your time, energy, and talents to matter on an eternal level, you must make the choice to live for God, to live for heaven, before you are inundated with the cares and ways of the world around you.

As you enter guided prayer, choose to engage God with the entirety of your heart. Don't just offer him action; offer him affection. Don't just bring the good parts of you, but come before him openly and honestly. Experience what it's like to be met with the reward of God's unconditional love and grace.

Notes:

GUIDED PRAYER

1. Meditate on the truth of God's word. Allow Scripture to fill you with a desire to store up the treasure of your heart in heaven.

   "Do not lay up for yourselves treasures on earth, where moth and rust destroy and where thieves break in and steal, but lay up for yourselves treasures in heaven, where neither moth nor rust destroys and where thieves do not break in and steal. For where your treasure is, there your heart will be also" (Matthew 6:19–21).

2. In what ways are you laying up treasure on earth? Where are you seeking fulfillment and provision from the world rather than God? What parts of your life are not God's best for you? What parts of your life won't produce an eternal reward?

3. Come before God openly and honestly. Give him your heart. Tell him how you feel and how you're doing. Ask him for the grace to sense his response. Rest in an experience with God's manifest presence and receive his grace.

   "Come to me, all who labor and are heavy laden, and I will give you rest. Take my yoke upon you, and learn from me, for I am gentle and lowly in heart, and you will find rest for your souls. For my yoke is easy, and my burden is light" (Matthew 11:28–30).

GO . . .

Oswald Chambers wrote in *My Utmost for His Highest*, "Joy means the perfect fulfillment of that for which I was created and regenerated." You were created and regenerated for unhindered communion with your heavenly Father. Experiencing true joy in this life will be the result of casting aside anything that chains your heart to this world. Live today for God alone and discover the wealth of life that comes from storing up your treasure in heaven.

Living from Value

WEEKLY OVERVIEW

In our first week of *Catalyst*, we'll explore seven answers to the heart's most important question: "Why?" Until we understand why spending time alone with God every day is worth the time and energy it takes, we'll never be able to develop consistency or go as deep into God's presence as we were created for. May you realize both the depth of your need and the goodness and availability of your Father as you discover your *why*.

SCRIPTURE

"Fear not, therefore; you are of more value than many sparrows" (Matthew 10:31).

DEVOTIONAL

A powerful by-product of time alone with God is discovering that we are valuable enough for God to meet with. If our Creator cares enough for us to speak to us, to give us a sense of his presence, to take our burdens and give us peace, then no man and no devil can tell us that we're not valuable. If God tells us that we're loved, then that means we are lovable. And what's more, when Jesus took on flesh and died on the cross, he communicated the depth of God's love for us once and for all. God so longed for a restored relationship with you that he sent his only Son to pay the highest price for your sin.

Even though the reality of Jesus' life, death, and resurrection is so foundational, so central to my faith, I find I need to be reminded of it every day if I am to experience the fullness of its fruit. I am so quick to believe that I'm worthless when I do the first thing wrong. I'm so prone to listen to and believe what the world says rather than tuning my ear to the still, small voice of my heavenly Father.

> *We aren't meant to live seeking our value from the world around us.*

Spending time alone with God every morning reminds me of my value. It fills me with the courage I need to live from a place of understanding my true value, of seeing myself as God sees me. Every morning, I need the Lord to speak over me in a fresh way the words, *"Fear not . . . you are of more value than many sparrows"* (Matthew 10:31).

Experiencing God's presence reminds me every morning that true satisfaction is only found in abiding with God and equips me to live fulfilled instead of seeking fulfillment in the world. Experiencing heaven come to earth reminds me that I am not home here and gives me peace no matter what trials come my way. Responding to God's love with my own love helps me to worship God alone and place no idol before him.

We aren't meant to live seeking our value from the world around us. We were meant to live from the revelation that we are already valuable enough for God to give his life for us no matter what we do or say.

Take time today in guided prayer to discover how immensely valuable you are to God. Search his heart and find that he so longed for a relationship with you—specifically you—that he would send his only Son to die just to have you. Allow a sense of God-worth to spring up within you that all striving for value from the world would cease in light of God's limitless love.

Notes:

GUIDED PRAYER

1. Meditate on John 3:16. Think about what this verse really means for you, of how immense God's love is specifically for you.

   "For God so loved the world, that he gave his only Son, that whoever believes in him should not perish but have eternal life" (John 3:16).

2. Where has the world told you that you're not valuable? Where are you striving to prove to others that you're worth something? Bring it all before God and lay it at his feet.

3. Ask God for a revelation of how valuable you are to him. Ask him how he feels about you. Take a moment to listen to whatever he would say. Pay attention to any sense you get. And rest in the revelation of your value to God.

   "Are not two sparrows sold for a penny? And not one of them will fall to the ground apart from your Father. But even the hairs of your head are all numbered. Fear not, therefore; you are of more value than many sparrows" (Matthew 10:29–31).

GO . . .

Think of how much more you could offer the world if you were able to live from a daily revelation of your intrinsic value to God. You weren't made to live apart from the truth that you're valuable. If you're not receiving that revelation from God, you'll seek to receive it from the world. Discovering your value to God every morning is foundational to loving others well; therefore, it is foundational to advancing God's kingdom. May you find peace in God's unconditional love and rest from the need to prove your worth to the world around you. And may you bear eternal fruit as you love others without the need to receive anything in return.

Eliminating the Should

WEEKLY OVERVIEW

In our first week of *Catalyst*, we'll explore seven answers to the heart's most important question: "Why?" Until we understand why spending time alone with God every day is worth the time and energy it takes, we'll never be able to develop consistency or go as deep into God's presence as we were created for. May you realize both the depth of your need and the goodness and availability of your Father as you discover your *why*.

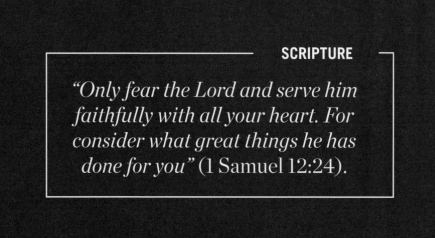

SCRIPTURE

"Only fear the Lord and serve him faithfully with all your heart. For consider what great things he has done for you" (1 Samuel 12:24).

The more responsibilities I get in life, the more I've begun to despise the word *should*. If we allow it to, life will pile on a bunch of *shoulds* until all our joy, spontaneity, and personality have been smothered out entirely. Sometimes, even our relationship with God can feel more like a *should* than a want. We *should* give; we *should* go to church; we *should* spend time alone with God. Pretty soon, God starts to seem a lot more like a taskmaster than a loving Father.

> *If we allow it to, life will pile on a bunch of shoulds until all our joy, spontaneity, and personality have been smothered out entirely.*

The more consistently I draw near to the true heart of God, the quicker I am learning that he's not that way at all. In fact, Scripture is filled with God speaking of his desire to be wanted by his people. Psalm 27:8 serves as a model of a truer way of seeking God: *"You have said, 'Seek my face.' My heart says to you, 'Your face, Lord, do I seek.'"*

Seeking God was always designed to be a response to his seeking of us. Our love is meant to be reciprocated, not manufactured. The last thing God wants to be is another *should*. His plan is to love you so often and so well that you can't help but love him back. His desire is to reveal how near he is to you and how full his heart is for you that you can't help but want to spend time alone with him.

Take time today to discover what *shoulds* have crept into your relationship with God that didn't really come from the Father at all. And make space to discover that you were made to dwell in the presence of God. May your heart be filled with devotion for God as you respond to his present and perfect love.

Notes:

GUIDED PRAYER

1. What parts of your relationship with God feel more like a *should* than a want? Take a moment to reflect and write them down.

2. Ask God for a revelation of his love and pursuit of you. Meditate on what Scripture says about God's unwavering love toward you.

   "There is no fear in love, but perfect love casts out fear. For fear has to do with punishment, and whoever fears has not been perfected in love. We love because he first loved us" (1 John 4:18–19).

3. Respond to the reality of God's love with your own love toward him. Cast down any *shoulds* at the feet of your loving Father. Thank him for what he's done for you. Thank him for his Son. Thank him for the Holy Spirit. And reflect on how good it is to have a real, eternal relationship with a God who is love.

   "Anyone who does not love does not know God, because God is love" (1 John 4:8).

   "Enter his gates with thanksgiving, and his courts with praise! Give thanks to him; bless his name! For the Lord is good; his steadfast love endures forever, and his faithfulness to all generations" (Psalm 100:4–5).

GO . . .

God would much rather you seek him with honesty than seek him with words or actions you don't mean. He can take your honesty. He won't turn away from you. He won't stop loving you. Coming before God with honesty opens your heart to receive his love in a real way, in a way you need. If you don't feel like doing something you know you should, talk to him about it! Ask him for the revelation you need to live your life wholeheartedly. You were made for everything God asks of you. Everything he leads you to is good. May today mark an important step forward in your journey to wholehearted, abundant living, a journey free from *shoulds* and filled with desire for the life God has so lovingly laid before you.

WEEK

How?

TWO

Forming Good Habits

WEEKLY OVERVIEW

In our first week of *Catalyst*, we looked at why spending time alone with God is so vital in experiencing all God has for us in this life. This week, we'll look at how to spend time alone with God. We'll explore principles and rhythms that, when adopted, have the power to produce amazing, life-giving fruit each day. May your mind and heart be awakened to the glory of all God has for you as you discover simple rhythms and principles of spending time alone with him.

SCRIPTURE

"For in him all the fullness of God was pleased to dwell, and through him to reconcile to himself all things, whether on earth or in heaven, making peace by the blood of his cross. And you, who once were alienated and hostile in mind, doing evil deeds, he has now reconciled in his body of flesh by his death, in order to present you holy and blameless and above reproach before him" (Colossians 1:19–22).

DEVOTIONAL

Imagine what your life would look like if spending time alone with God in the first moments of your day were a habit for you. Imagine the peace, freedom, and love you would experience if each day began with a fresh revelation of God's nearness and unconditional love.

For a long time, I thought habits were for the disciplined—the regimented. I've always thought of myself as fairly spontaneous. Left to my own devices, I stay up late and live based on how I feel at the moment instead of what I've predetermined is best for me. But the reality is, we all have habits. We're habitual beings whether we like to admit it or not.

In *The Power of Habit,* Charles Duhigg cites a 2006 study published by a Duke University researcher that proved, on average, 40% of the actions people perform on any given day are done by habit. Duhigg goes on to make a powerful, compelling case that habits can be formed and changed if we understand what a habit is comprised of and take educated action to develop or change that habit.[1]

As we're looking this week at principles and rhythms that when adopted will produce life-giving fruit, what better place to begin than by learning how we can form the habit of spending time alone with God every morning.

Duhigg states that a habit loop is comprised of three elements:

1. A **cue** is a trigger for an action.
2. A **ritual** is the action itself.
3. The **reward** is why we act in the first place, the reason a habit is formed.

An example is the cue of hunger, the action of making and eating a sandwich, and the reward of feeling full—pretty simple stuff. What's important is understanding that a habit is only truly formed once we begin to crave a reward. It has to be done long enough for our body to experience, remember, and begin to crave a reward, so, when we're cued, we actually feel a sense of reward before we even act.

In exercising, for instance, once we get a consistent taste of the endorphins released after working out, the body will begin to crave exercising. When a habit is formed, an impression is left in the brain, a groove that makes it easier and easier to take the same action and receive the reward once we're cued. As God's people, when we take his heart to lead us to abundant life and align that with a proper, practical understanding of how our mind and body works, powerful habits can be formed.

Colossians 1:19–22 says:

> *For in him all the fullness of God was pleased to dwell, and through him to reconcile to himself all things, whether on earth or in heaven, making peace by the blood of his cross. And you, who once were alienated and hostile in mind, doing evil deeds, he has now reconciled in his body of flesh by his death, in order to present you holy and blameless and above reproach before him.*

> *The most practical, powerful habit we can form to center our lives around the reality of God's goodness is to spend time alone with him every day.*

God longs to redeem those habits that are keeping us from experiencing abundant life and help us form habits that position us to receive all the wonderful gifts he longs to give us. The most practical, powerful habit we can form to center our lives around the reality of God's goodness is to spend time alone with him every day.

Practically, the path to spending time alone with God every morning could look like this:

1. **Create a cue every morning that will trigger the ritual of spending time alone with God.** The cue could be setting your alarm to a worship song, setting your Bible by your bed, leaving your journal and Bible open and read, or setting your coffee pot to brew at the time you set aside to meet with God. Decide on a time and cue you can be consistent with so that the habit can have an opportunity to form.

2. **Act on your cue with the ritual of spending time alone with God.** We created this book to give you a consistent way to meet with God as you're seeking to develop or strengthen this habit. Later this week, we'll talk about a rhythm you can develop to maximize the life-giving ritual of time alone with God. The main goal with your ritual is spending time alone with God in a way that produces a reward for you every morning.

3. **Receive your reward every day you meet with God.** Last week, we looked at some amazing rewards God has in store for you as you make space to meet with him. God longs to speak value over you, illuminate your identity, and lavish his love and affection on you. As you make room to receive the amazing gifts God has in store for you, you will begin to crave your time alone with your heavenly Father. If you're not getting a sense of reward from your time alone with God, take time to think about why! Maybe you need to add something to your time or take something away. Maybe you need to ask God for a fresh revelation of his plans for meeting with you. As you grow in developing an effective time with the Father, the life-giving habit of spending time alone with him will form naturally because you were made to dwell in God's presence.

Take time today as we pray to reflect on how life-giving it would be to meet with your Father every day. Make room for the Holy Spirit to reveal a cue that would be effective for you. Set your heart on the rewards God longs to give you. And allow today to serve as a catalyst for this rhythm of meeting with God that will satisfy your heart for years and years to come.

Notes:

GUIDED PRAYER

1. Ask the Holy Spirit to give you a sense of what he has in store for you as you make space to meet with him. Ask him what reward he longs to give you. Think about things he's done in the past as you met with him. Maybe you gained wisdom. Maybe you had a sense of peace or fulfillment. Ponder on those rewards for a few moments.

   "Every good gift and every perfect gift is from above, coming down from the Father of lights with whom there is no variation or shadow due to change" (James 1:17).

   "If any of you lacks wisdom, let him ask God, who gives generously to all without reproach, and it will be given him" (James 1:5).

   "Now may the Lord of peace himself give you peace at all times in every way. The Lord be with you all" (2 Thessalonians 3:16).

2. Ask God to give you an idea of an effective cue for your time alone with him. What can you set as a visual cue, a reminder to spend time alone with God? The goal is to find something you can be consistent with.

3. Ask God for the grace to develop this habit of meeting with him. Take time to allow your heart to be filled with grace and courage that you can do this. There is nothing truly in the way of you meeting with God every morning. If others can do it, you can do it. If God is calling you to a daily experience with his presence, he will give you the grace and help you need to answer that call.

   "The steadfast love of the Lord never ceases; his mercies never come to an end; they are new every morning; great is your faithfulness. 'The Lord is my portion,' says my soul, 'therefore I will hope in him'" (Lamentations 3:22–24).

GO . . .

No matter how many times you've picked up and let go of the rhythm of spending time alone with God, know that God's mercies are new every morning. Every day is a new opportunity to meet with your Father. Every day you have new need of God, and he has fresh gifts he longs to give you. God's not condemning you for what you did yesterday. Rather, he's drawing you into a fresh opportunity to experience his love and redemption today. May you be strengthened and encouraged in your desire to spend time alone with God.

Choose a Time

WEEKLY OVERVIEW

In our first week of *Catalyst*, we looked at why spending time alone with God is so vital in experiencing all God has for us in this life. This week, we'll look at how to spend time alone with God. We'll explore principles and rhythms that, when adopted, have the power to produce amazing, life-giving fruit each day. May your mind and heart be awakened to the glory of all God has for you as you discover simple rhythms and principles of spending time alone with him.

"Look carefully then how you walk, not as unwise but as wise, making the best use of the time, because the days are evil" (Ephesians 5:15–16).

DEVOTIONAL

One of the most challenging aspects of developing the rhythm of spending time alone with God can be making room to meet with him in an already busy day. Modern living is filled with countless opportunities for ways you can spend your time. More entertainment is created than an individual could reasonably consume. Social media brims with more engaging content than anyone could catch up with. People all around us are working, studying, learning, and striving toward success at all times of the day. Time, our most precious resource, only seems to become more and more valuable.

One of my greatest struggles in developing the rhythm of spending time alone with God was actualizing the desire in my heart to meet with my heavenly Father. I would wake up with the desire and assume I would find time later to meet with God. But, inevitably, my day would get filled up with things that seemed so pressing and so urgent that I wouldn't make space to meet with God. I learned that simply having the desire to meet with God often wasn't enough. I had to take practical steps toward actualizing the desire in my heart.

Because our lives are so busy, choosing to say yes to meeting with God means you have to say no to something else. We can't squeeze every opportunity into every day. And the most practical step you can take to develop the habit of meeting with God is to pick a time that works for you and guard that time.

Moses prayed in Psalm 90:12, *"So teach us to number our days that we may get a heart of wisdom."* God has too much in store for you to put off meeting with him one day. Because spending time alone with God is foundational to living the life God longs to give us, our set-aside time must be our priority. Experiencing God is more important than time spent on entertainment or social media. Spending time with God is more important even than time with friends or family. It's not that any of those things are wrong; it's just that time alone with God makes every other part of life better, richer, and marked by the abundance Jesus died to give you. Time alone with God is the foundation on which the rest of life is meant to be built.

For me, the first thing in the morning is the only time I can really be consistent. Carving out time at the very beginning of my day means that no opportunity can surprise me and rob me of my time alone with God. It also has the added benefit of allowing my whole day to be built on an experience with the love and leadership of God.

> *Because our lives are so busy, choosing to say yes to meeting with God means you have to say no to someone else.*

As we enter a time of guided prayer today, pick a time you can consistently meet with God. Ask the Holy Spirit for wisdom. Allow God's desire to meet with you to shift your priorities. Choose to center your life around your relationship with God. Watch as peace and love flood your days. And may your time alone with God result in blessing and life in every other moment.

Notes:

GUIDED PRAYER

1. Take a moment and ask the Lord what he wants to accomplish in your heart as you develop this rhythm of meeting with him. God doesn't want to add another thing you should do in your life. He wants to meet with you because it's the best thing for you. He wants to lead you to a lifestyle of desiring to meet with him.

   "Bless the Lord, O my soul, and forget not all his benefits, who forgives all your iniquity, who heals all your diseases, who redeems your life from the pit, who crowns you with steadfast love and mercy, who satisfies you with good so that your youth is renewed like the eagle's" (Psalm 103:2–5).

2. What's in your way of meeting with God every day? Are there one or two things you're spending your time on now that crowds out your time alone with God? Highlight what they are and lay them before God's feet in prayer.

   "Take my yoke upon you, and learn from me, for I am gentle and lowly in heart, and you will find rest for your souls" (Matthew 11:29).

3. Ask the Holy Spirit to give you wisdom on a time you can set aside to meet with God. Take a moment and think about the normal rhythm of your day. When can you be most consistent? Rather than squeezing time alone with God into everything else you've already committed to, prioritize God first.

   "But seek first the kingdom of God and his righteousness, and all these things will be added to you" (Matthew 6:33).

GO . . .

God's heart is never for you to beat yourself up. In life, you will grow and develop. New opportunities and challenges will come. If a rhythm isn't working for you, change it! No one is in control of your life but you. God has given you what you need to choose him. Fight for what you want your life to look like. Fight to create space to experience the love and grace of your heavenly Father. Don't let the world entice you away from what you were made for: the presence of God. May you find the strength and grace you need to root your life in God as you experience wave after wave of his goodness.

Develop a Rhythm

WEEKLY OVERVIEW

In our first week of *Catalyst*, we looked at why spending time alone with God is so vital in experiencing all God has for us in this life. This week, we'll look at how to spend time alone with God. We'll explore principles and rhythms that, when adopted, have the power to produce amazing, life-giving fruit each day. May your mind and heart be awakened to the glory of all God has for you as you discover simple rhythms and principles of spending time alone with him.

SCRIPTURE

"Blessed is the man [whose] delight is in the law of the Lord, and on his law he meditates day and night. He is like a tree planted by streams of water that yields its fruit in its season, and its leaf does not wither. In all that he does, he prospers" (Psalm 1:1–3).

DEVOTIONAL

Across the next four devotionals, we'll unpack a rhythm that's been the most life-giving to me in my time alone with God: be honest, worship, read, and pray. But for today, I want to explore the concept and value of having a rhythm to our time alone with God.

For years, my time alone with God felt all over the place, if I managed even to have one at all. I knew I should be reading the Bible. I knew I should pray. I honestly never even thought about worshiping outside of a congregational setting. I saw that other people journaled but never really understood why.

And beyond not understanding the true value of the individual elements, I had a hard time spending time alone with God at all if I wasn't sure what I was going to do. The hurdle of having not only to make time to meet with God but also deciding what to do in my time was sometimes too high to climb when there were plenty of other things I could spend my time on.

So, when I got really serious about wanting to meet with God every day, I found that developing a consistent rhythm was a critical part of getting the most out of my time alone with God. Also, having the question answered of what I was going to spend my time doing was a huge help in developing consistency.

> *For me, the rhythm every day of being honest, worshiping, reading, and praying created spaces in which I could pursue and experience God in fresh and life-giving ways every morning.*

Good rhythms should never negatively limit you. Rather, the goal is to fashion something that's sturdy enough to create healthy boundaries but flexible enough to allow for spontaneity. For me, the rhythm every day of being honest, worshiping, reading, and praying created spaces in which I could pursue and experience God in fresh and life-giving ways every morning. It created a framework in which I could be spontaneous and implement different worship songs, readings, and styles of prayer, all the while keeping me from spending my time I've set aside to meet with God just figuring out what to do.

As we enter guided prayer, take a moment to seek God's heart on rhythm. Think about how a rhythm to your time alone with him might help you. And take some time to think about the elements of meeting with God that have been and would be the most fruitful in your life.

Notes:

GUIDED PRAYER

1. Reflect for a moment on the benefits of creating a framework for experiencing God. Allow your desire to be stirred to create spaces that God can fill with his life-giving presence.

2. What elements of meeting with God have been most fruitful in your life? What do you most enjoy about getting time alone with God? What are the reasons you want to meet with God in the first place? Take a moment to journal your thoughts.

3. What could a rhythm to meeting with God look like for you? What would help you get the most out of the time you set aside? As a reference, what would it be like to start with the four elements of being honest, worshiping, reading, and praying? Across the next few days, we'll unpack the value of each of those elements. But for today, think and pray about what would be most helpful to you.

GO . . .

Our time is too valuable not to get the most out of whatever we spend it on.
Your time alone with God is your own! There's no need to be religious about
it. The goal is not checking off a box but building a relationship. Creating a
rhythm out of desire and grace rather than obligation is the only way that
rhythm will be effective. And your rhythm can grow as you grow. May any
rhythm you develop be birthed out of God's grace and patience working
within you to help you develop a habit that will infuse your day with identity,
purpose, love, and peace.

Be Honest

WEEKLY OVERVIEW

In our first week of *Catalyst*, we looked at why spending time alone with God is so vital in experiencing all God has for us in this life. This week, we'll look at how to spend time alone with God. We'll explore principles and rhythms that, when adopted, have the power to produce amazing, life-giving fruit each day. May your mind and heart be awakened to the glory of all God has for you as you discover simple rhythms and principles of spending time alone with him.

SCRIPTURE

"Righteous lips are the delight of a king, and he loves him who speaks what is right" (Proverbs 16:13).

DEVOTIONAL

I've spent countless, exhausting hours in my fleeting life working to portray myself as a person I know I'm not. Whether in relationships with friends, family, my spouse, or God, I find myself consistently creating a facade I hope others will like better than who I actually am. I fear that if I truly open myself up to others and get rejected, I will have nothing left. If I am fully myself, will I be enough?

Hebrews 4:13 says, *"And no creature is hidden from his sight, but all are naked and exposed to the eyes of him to whom we must give account."* Scriptures like this used to seriously frighten me. The idea that an all-powerful, all-knowing, and perfectly holy God knew everything I had ever done was too invasive for me. If I couldn't even muster up the courage to truly be myself to others, how could I handle being *"naked and exposed"* to my heavenly Father?

It wasn't until I began experiencing the powerful, overwhelming love of my heavenly Father that these frail, false constructions began to fall apart brick by brick, lie after lie. The process God takes us through in unveiling our hearts represents his perfect kindness, patience, and pursuit of us. He waits for us to come before him openly and honestly, patiently beckoning us with his love. He is perfectly accepting of us as long as we don't fake it with him. As soon as the Prodigal Son came home in a posture of humility and honesty, he was immediately embraced, accepted, and offered an authentic relationship with his father once again.

It's absolutely vital that we pursue honesty before God because he will not address what is not real and not true. He will not try and help this false projection we make become an even better facade. He will not meet with that which doesn't truly exist. Brennan Manning writes in his book *Abba's Child: The Cry of the Heart for Intimate Belonging,* "The false self is frustrated because he never hears God's voice. He cannot, since God sees no one there."[2] Thomas Merton says of the false self, "This is the man I want myself to be but who cannot exist, because God does not know anything about him."

To be honest before God is to invite a perfectly loving, powerful, and grace-filled Father into the places of our lives that need him the most. Honesty is the place to begin every time you meet with God. If we jump straight into worshiping, reading, or praying without first being honest, we're in danger of missing an experience with God altogether. God longs to be asked into the very wounds we work so tirelessly to cover. He longs to heal and transform the darkest, hardest places of our hearts into fertile soil that can bear the fruit of his Spirit. He longs for us to be fully known by him in every way that we might experience the full depths of his powerful, transformational love.

> *It's absolutely vital that we pursue honesty before God because he will not address what is not real and not true.*

Take time in guided prayer to truly open your heart to God and be honest. Tell him your doubts, fears, and failures. Open before him the parts of your past you have worked so hard to cover. And let his love in that you might experience healing today in his powerful presence.

Notes:

GUIDED PRAYER

1. Meditate on the importance of being honest before God. Ask the Holy Spirit to fill you with courage to be vulnerable before God in faith.

   "And no creature is hidden from his sight, but all are naked and exposed to the eyes of him to whom we must give account" (Hebrews 4:13).

   "Would not God discover this? For he knows the secrets of the heart" (Psalm 44:21).

2. Open your heart to God and be truly honest with him. How are you feeling right now? What parts of your life do you feel tempted to ignore, to shove aside, to hide? Ask the Holy Spirit to reveal any places of your heart that are veiled and kept in shadows.

3. Ask God to help you receive his love in the areas of your heart that are in desperate need of him. Reveal to him the places of your past that have plagued you for so long. Take courage and bring before your loving, powerful Father that which is keeping you from a truly abundant life. Ask God how he feels about you that you might receive healing.

   "He heals the brokenhearted and binds up their wounds" (Psalm 147:3).

GO . . .

Making space in our lives to receive healing for our hearts from the Lord is a vital exercise in spiritual growth. We don't have to be plagued by wounds from our past. We don't have to spend so much of our energy trying to cover those times we were genuinely hurt. The only path to growth passes through God's healing presence. He wants to address and heal that which you might feel has formed you. He wants to tear up all the work you've done to harden your heart that you might truly live healed, free, and vulnerable. Pursue healing for your heart and experience the life available to you in the power of the Holy Spirit.

Worship

WEEKLY OVERVIEW

In our first week of *Catalyst*, we looked at why spending time alone with God is so vital in experiencing all God has for us in this life. This week, we'll look at how to spend time alone with God. We'll explore principles and rhythms that, when adopted, have the power to produce amazing, life-giving fruit each day. May your mind and heart be awakened to the glory of all God has for you as you discover simple rhythms and principles of spending time alone with him.

SCRIPTURE

"Therefore let us be grateful for receiving a kingdom that cannot be shaken, and thus let us offer to God acceptable worship, with reverence and awe" (Hebrews 12:28).

DEVOTIONAL

It's so easy for my time alone with God to be all about myself. I have so many problems, questions, and needs that if I'm not careful, I easily become the center of my time rather than God. Worship is a consistent reminder that life is only good when Jesus is at the center. When I take time to center myself around God's glory and goodness through worship, everything else seems to come into perspective. When I see and experience the glory of God, when I sing of his power and love, the cares and weights of the world begin to pale in comparison to the goodness and glory of Jesus.

Often, it's really tempting to jump past worship straight into praying, reading, or journaling. The results of worship often don't seem as quantifiable. But worship is foundational to experiencing God every morning. When we worship, we position ourselves in a place of trusting that God already knows our needs before we ask him (Matthew 6:8) and that his heart is truly for us (Romans 8:31). As we worship, we align our thoughts and emotions with the reality of God's power and love and receive the peace that comes through faith and trust alone.

> *When I take time to center myself around God's glory and goodness through worship, everything else seems to come into perspective.*

So, after taking time to be honest before God, I always try to engage in authentic worship. Depending on my environment, I'll sing or just listen, and often just for a song or two. It's amazing how worship can become a well-worn path to God's presence. Every morning, regardless of the state of my heart, the Lord draws me into his love and softens my heart as I worship. As I engage with a song, I seem to let my guard down, my mind seems to be more at ease, and I can truly experience God with my heart.

Hebrews 12:28 says, *"Therefore let us be grateful for receiving a kingdom that cannot be shaken, and thus let us offer to God acceptable worship, with reverence and awe."* Take time today in guided prayer to reflect on the value of worship. Allow God to reveal the power of coming before him in song. Choose today to engage with God in worship so that God will be at the center of your heart and that your life will bear the fruit of sustaining peace and eternal purpose.

Notes:

GUIDED PRAYER

1. Meditate on the power and value of worship. Allow Scripture to stir up your heart to engage with God through song every day.

   "But the hour is coming, and is now here, when the true worshipers will worship the Father in spirit and truth, for the Father is seeking such people to worship him" (John 4:23).

   "Therefore let us be grateful for receiving a kingdom that cannot be shaken, and thus let us offer to God acceptable worship, with reverence and awe" (Hebrews 12:28).

2. Ask God for a revelation of the power of worship. Ask him why he wants you specifically to worship.

3. Choose today to engage in a song of worship. Whether right now, in your car, or later in your home, choose to be a doer of the word and declare God's glory in the earth through song.

   "My heart is steadfast, O God, my heart is steadfast! I will sing and make melody!" (Psalm 57:7).

   "I will sing to the Lord, because he has dealt bountifully with me" (Psalm 13:6).

GO . . .

Worshiping through song isn't just for the musically inclined. First Samuel 16:7 says that the Lord looks at the heart. He loves when you come before him in song because of how beautiful it is to him for you to worship with your heart, regardless of what you sound like. Worship can feel so unnatural to us sometimes because it's a heavenly act. So, choosing to engage in worship here on earth has a unique power, a heavenly effect on us. May you engage in the rhythm of daily worship and experience its profound, heavenly effect on your heart and life.

Read

WEEKLY OVERVIEW

In our first week of *Catalyst*, we looked at why spending time alone with God is so vital in experiencing all God has for us in this life. This week, we'll look at how to spend time alone with God. We'll explore principles and rhythms that, when adopted, have the power to produce amazing, life-giving fruit each day. May your mind and heart be awakened to the glory of all God has for you as you discover simple rhythms and principles of spending time alone with him.

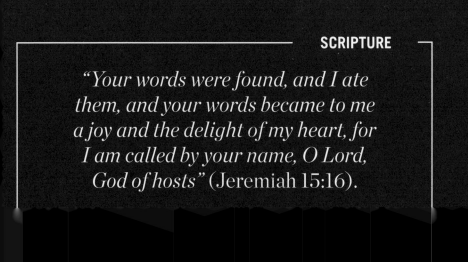

SCRIPTURE

"Your words were found, and I ate them, and your words became to me a joy and the delight of my heart, for I am called by your name, O Lord, God of hosts" (Jeremiah 15:16).

DEVOTIONAL

God has given us an incredible gift in authoring and preserving his word. We have the very words of God, spoken in perfect wisdom, at our fingertips. We have the story of creation, the fall, and redemption offered to us by the Author of history, the Creator of all. When we faithfully read, meditate, and respond to his word, he promises that our lives will be marked by the blessing and favor of heaven (Proverbs 3).

Even more amazing than the fact that we have God's word is that he's filled us with the Holy Spirit, the very Author himself. We don't have to read Scripture and then understand and act on our own. As we read, the Spirit longs to be with us, reveal the heart behind his words, and guide us to unique and perfect action.

After taking time to come before God openly and honestly in worship, we should devote ourselves to the reading of Scripture in communion with the Holy Spirit. We should give ourselves to the act of ruminating on God's truth, on real wisdom, that we might live our lives grounded in what is whole and good.

> *His intention isn't that the Bible would replace meeting with him face-to-face but rather be an aid to abiding in his presence in truth and in wisdom.*

For too long, I misunderstood how to read God's word, and therefore it always felt like a cold obligation. I didn't make space for the Spirit to speak when I read. I read the Bible like a textbook on life written by an author who doesn't know my situation, who left all the application up to me. But God longs for his word to be an avenue to experiencing him. His intention isn't that the Bible would replace meeting with him face-to-face but rather be an aid to abiding in his presence in truth and in wisdom.

Hebrews 4:12 tells us that God's word is *"living and active."* As we enter guided prayer, make space to allow Scripture to fill you with life and action and to lead you to the presence of its Author. Proverbs 3:13–14 says, *"Blessed is the one who finds wisdom, and the one who gets understanding, for the gain from her is better than gain from silver and her profit better than gold."* May your heart be filled with the wisdom of the Father today, that your life would be marked by the riches if inward abundance found only in authentic relationship with the one true God.

Notes:

GUIDED PRAYER

1. Take time to reflect on the goodness of what's available to you in Scripture. Thank God for making his word so readily available to you.

   "Your words were found, and I ate them, and your words became to me a joy and the delight of my heart, for I am called by your name, O Lord, God of hosts" (Jeremiah 15:16).

   "My son, be attentive to my words; incline your ear to my sayings. Let them not escape from your sight; keep them within your heart. For they are life to those who find them, and healing to all their flesh. Keep your heart with all vigilance, for from it flow the springs of life" (Proverbs 4:20–23).

2. Now take time to thank God for filling you with his Spirit. Ask the Spirit to reveal his presence to you. Ask him to guide you as you spend time in his word.

   "If you love me, you will keep my commandments. And I will ask the Father, and he will give you another Helper, to be with you forever, even the Spirit of truth, whom the world cannot receive, because it neither sees him nor knows him. You know him, for he dwells with you and will be in you" (John 14:15–17).

3. Take time to meditate on Joshua 1:8–9. Allow the Holy Spirit to reveal what he has for you today in his word. Ask him what in your life should change as a response. And commit to being a doer of God's word.

   "This Book of the Law shall not depart from your mouth, but you shall meditate on it day and night, so that you may be careful to do according to all that is written in it. For then you will make your way prosperous, and then you will have good success. Have I not commanded you? Be strong and courageous. Do not be frightened, and do not be dismayed, for the Lord your God is with you wherever you go" (Joshua 1:8–9).

GO . . .

Getting in the habit of daily Scripture reading is a process. Habits aren't formed overnight. Have grace for yourself. Seek God through his word as often as you can. Return to his word no matter how many days it's been since you've read it. God doesn't look at you with condemnation but with grace and love. He's simply excited to speak to you whenever you'll listen. May God's grace draw you in as you seek him.

Pray

WEEKLY OVERVIEW

In our first week of *Catalyst*, we looked at why spending time alone with God is so vital in experiencing all God has for us in this life. This week, we'll look at how to spend time alone with God. We'll explore principles and rhythms that, when adopted, have the power to produce amazing, life-giving fruit each day. May your mind and heart be awakened to the glory of all God has for you as you discover simple rhythms and principles of spending time alone with him.

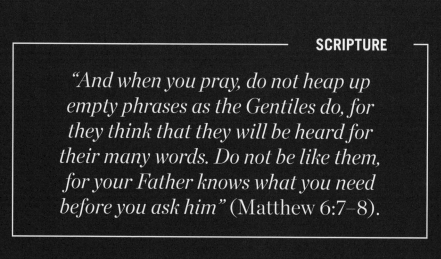

SCRIPTURE

"And when you pray, do not heap up empty phrases as the Gentiles do, for they think that they will be heard for their many words. Do not be like them, for your Father knows what you need before you ask him" (Matthew 6:7–8).

DEVOTIONAL

My time spent in direct communication with God is often when my life is most changed. Honesty, worship, and reading are amazing ways to begin my time with God. But ensuring that they lead to time where I'm able to ask God the questions burning in my heart, or to make space simply to listen to whatever he wants to say, is vital to experiencing the richness of relationship God longs to have with me.

Oswald Chambers said, "We think of prayer as a preparation for work, or a calm after having done work, whereas prayer is the essential work."[4]

> ## *"We think of prayer as a preparation for work, or a calm after having done work, whereas prayer is the essential work."*

It's in prayer that we discover and experience the personality of God. It's in prayer that we sense his heart, his motivations, his love. It's in prayer that we learn to hear God's still, small voice. And it's from hearing the still, small voice of God in prayer that we learn to recognize it when all the world around us is shouting.

Taking five minutes to let God speak, laying before him the weight on our hearts, and discovering that his burden is light are all vital, necessary investments if we long to bear the fruit of the Spirit. Prayer changes things. It changes us.

In Matthew 6:7–8, Jesus says, *"And when you pray, do not heap up empty phrases as the Gentiles do, for they think that they will be heard for their many words. Do not be like them, for your Father knows what you need before you ask him."* Your heavenly Father loves to listen to you. He cares deeply about what's weighing on your heart. And he's so good, so loving, and so filled with grace that all he needs is for you to open up, and he responds. It's not about the beauty of your language. It's not about the rightness of your words. It's about your honesty and faith and his unceasing love.

Take time to really listen to God today as you pray. And may the voice of your Father calm your fears, fill you with faith, and guide you to a posture of abiding in the reality of his presence.

Notes:

GUIDED PRAYER

1. Reflect on the reality that God is listening. The ear of your Creator is open to you.

   "Then you will call upon me and come and pray to me, and I will hear you" (Jeremiah 29:12).

   "And this is the confidence that we have toward him, that if we ask anything according to his will he hears us" (1 John 5:14).

2. Bring before God anything that's weighing on your heart. Tell him how you feel or what you're worried about. And be still before him, acknowledging that he hears your prayer.

   "Humble yourselves, therefore, under the mighty hand of God so that at the proper time he may exalt you, casting all your anxieties on him, because he cares for you" (1 Peter 5:6–7).

3. Now ask God to help you hear his response. Ask him what he thinks about your questions or concerns. Ask him how he feels about you. Pay attention to any way he might respond to you and find rest in his response.

GO . . .

The concept of God's voice being still and small always made me wonder why God would talk so quietly. Wouldn't everything be better if his voice rose above the chaos so I wouldn't miss it? But lately, the nature of God's voice has been serving as an amazing reminder of his nearness. God is so close to me that he never needs to speak above a whisper. He's always with me. He's in me. There is no reason to shout. As I tune my ear to this still, small voice, I find myself being drawn into deeper communion with my Father. I find him pulling me out of the chaos of the world and into the peace and life of abiding in him. May we as God's children learn to tune out the noise around us and find guidance, peace, and life in the stillness of our Father's voice.

WEEK

Get the Most

THREE

Set the Bar

WEEKLY OVERVIEW

Often, the biggest reason we struggle to meet with God consistently is that we don't know how to get the most out of our time alone with him. Last week in *Catalyst*, we learned some principles and rhythms on how to meet with God. This week, we'll explore how to get the most out of those principles and rhythms. May God give you a true glimpse this week of the immeasurable glory and goodness he has in store for you every morning you set aside time to meet with him.

SCRIPTURE

"If then you have been raised with Christ, seek the things that are above, where Christ is, seated at the right hand of God" (Colossians 3:1).

DEVOTIONAL

I find it so easy to settle in life. Whether it's my health, finances, marriage, or relationship with God, I always seem to settle for less than what God wants for me. Lately, I've been sensing his encouragement to set my bar higher. God is calling me to a lifestyle of never settling for less than all he longs to give me. In his call to set my bar higher, I'm learning that my life is far more symptomatic of what I've let myself receive from God than what he longs to give.

In John 10:7–10 Jesus says:

> *Truly, truly, I say to you, I am the door of the sheep. All who came before me are thieves and robbers, but the sheep did not listen to them. I am the door. If anyone enters by me, he will be saved and will go in and out and find pasture. The thief comes only to steal and kill and destroy. I came that they may have life and have it abundantly.*

Jesus' mission was to give us abundant life for all of eternity, and that includes right now. He died that we might be set free from the terrible hold of sin, be restored to communion with God, and experience the fruit of heaven coming to earth. But for our experience to line up with God's word, we must position ourselves to receive his amazing gifts. Just as the lost must choose to receive the free gift of salvation, you and I must choose to receive the wonderful gifts afforded to us by the sacrifice of Jesus. And positioning ourselves to receive those gifts begins by setting our bar higher, by settling for nothing less than all God has for us.

> *When we set our bar for our emotional health higher, we won't settle for lack of peace or joy.*

When we set the bar for our marriage higher, where God would have it, we won't settle for lack of connection, we won't settle for selfish motives, and we won't settle for lack of kingdom fruit. Instead, we'll fight until our marriage looks like one filled with the grace and power of God. When we set our bar for our emotional health higher, we won't settle for lack of peace or joy. Instead, we'll draw closer to the Holy Spirit until we experience the biblically stated fruit of his presence in our lives (Galatians 5:22–23).

And when we set our bar for our relationship with God higher, we won't settle for a life lived as if God didn't tear the veil at Jesus' death. We won't settle for lack of his presence, lack of his voice, lack of his guidance. Instead, we'll keep seeking until our lives are marked by continual communion, constant communication, and moment-by-moment leadership from our Good Shepherd.

Take time today in guided prayer to identify places where your bar should be set higher, ask God for a better picture of the life he has for you, and receive the grace to experience now the abundant life Jesus died to give you.

Notes:

GUIDED PRAYER

1. Where is your life not marked by abundance? Where are you not experiencing the fruit of the Spirit or the presence of God? Where do you feel like you're constantly striving in your own strength?

   "I came that they may have life and have it abundantly" (John 10:10).

   "But the fruit of the Spirit is love, joy, peace, patience, kindness, goodness, faithfulness, gentleness, self-control" (Galatians 5:22–23).

   "You make known to me the path of life; in your presence there is fullness of joy; at your right hand are pleasures forevermore" (Psalm 16:11).

2. Ask God for a clearer picture of what he has for you in that area. Ask him how he would have your life be more abundant. Take time to discover his heart today.

3. Ask the Holy Spirit for help in discerning what practical steps you can take today to set your bar higher. What's one thing you can do to experience more abundant life?

GO . . .

James 1:17 says, *"Every good gift and every perfect gift is from above, coming down from the Father of lights, with whom there is no variation or shadow due to change."* You have a good Father who loves to give you good gifts. He knows exactly what you need. He knows how you're wired. And he is the perfect one to lead you to abundant life. Trust in the guidance of your Good Shepherd. Set your eyes on him and follow him wherever he goes. Know that as you follow in faith, God will do far more than you could ever ask or imagine. He will bring heaven to earth all around you. Raise your bar in faith today in every area you can, and fight to live the life made available to you by Jesus' loving sacrifice.

Experiencing God's Presence

WEEKLY OVERVIEW

Often, the biggest reason we struggle to meet with God consistently is that we don't know how to get the most out of our time alone with him. Last week in *Catalyst*, we learned some principles and rhythms on how to meet with God. This week, we'll explore how to get the most out of those principles and rhythms. May God give you a true glimpse this week of the immeasurable glory and goodness he has in store for you every morning you set aside time to meet with him.

SCRIPTURE

"Draw near to God, and he will draw near to you" (James 4:8).

DEVOTIONAL

Experiencing the presence of God sounds like such a mystery. It sounds like this wonderful but evasive thing that some people feel sometimes but isn't concrete enough to expect or place your hope in. Often, we associate God's presence with emotions and music, as if it were a breeze so light and momentary you almost couldn't be sure it happened at all.

In reality, God's presence is as simple as being in the presence of a friend or spouse. It's as uncomplicated and concrete as being around a person, except for one truth: God never leaves. Just as you can be in the same room as a friend and not know it, you can live the Christian life apart from experiencing God's nearness. Just as you can be sitting right across from a friend and be so busy with technology or your own thoughts to truly acknowledge that he or she is there, you can go through life focused on the busyness of present circumstances and miss out on the reality that God is closer than your breath.

> *To seek God is to experience God.*

We can find hope for encountering the presence of God in Psalm 27:4. Scripture says, *"One thing have I asked of the Lord, that will I seek after: that I may dwell in the house of the Lord all the days of my life, to gaze upon the beauty of the Lord and to inquire in his temple."* This pursuit, this action of seeking the living God, never comes back empty. To seek God is to experience God. Emotions aside, complexities cast away—God is already with you. He is already closer than he could ever be. His Spirit, his presence on the earth, never leaves you and never forsakes you. And when you turn your attention toward him, just as you can to a friend sitting across a table from you, you can experience him.

Psalm 139:7 says, *"Where shall I go from your Spirit? Or where shall I flee from your presence?"* God's presence is always available. He's not a friend who turns away from you or hides his heart. He's not a small gust of wind that comes and goes as he pleases. He's a God who would suffer and die that he might tear the veil and make his presence fully, continuously available to all who would seek him. He's a God who's working tirelessly to restore his crown of creation to himself that we might walk with him like in the garden of Eden, but this time for all of eternity with no possibility of a fall or barrier between us.

Experiencing God's presence is as simple as turning your attention toward him and allowing yourself to be fully known by him. May you find true peace and rest today as you make space to experience the presence of your Creator.

Notes:

GUIDED PRAYER

1. Meditate on the availability of God's presence.

   "Where shall I go from your Spirit? Or where shall I flee from your presence?" (Psalm 139:7).

   "You will seek me and find me, when you seek me with all your heart" (Jeremiah 29:13).

   "Or do you not know that your body is a temple of the Holy Spirit within you, whom you have from God? You are not your own, for you were bought with a price" (1 Corinthians 6:19–20).

2. What's your greatest distraction from experiencing God's presence? What thing, what belief, what pursuit holds you back from truly abiding in God?

3. Surrender that distraction to God right now. Choose to seek him first today. Let go of anything that holds you back from the richness of relationship God created you for.

   "One thing have I asked of the Lord, that will I seek after: that I may dwell in the house of the Lord all the days of my life, to gaze upon the beauty of the Lord and to inquire in his temple" (Psalm 27:4).

GO . . .

God's goal is for communion with you, and he won't settle for anything less. He's guiding you to a lifestyle of meeting with him. You were made for communion with your Creator. You were made to abide in God. Resting in God's presence is as natural as breathing and more life-giving than anything you've ever experienced. God is already with you. He never leaves you. Learning how to acknowledge his presence in every part of life is a journey filled with revelation, growth, and abundance. May you seek to dwell in the house of the Lord all your days and in every way, that your heart would be filled with God's goodness and restored to the true reason you were created: real relationship with your heavenly Father.

Hearing God's Voice

WEEKLY OVERVIEW

Often, the biggest reason we struggle to meet with God consistently is that we don't know how to get the most out of our time alone with him. Last week in *Catalyst*, we learned some principles and rhythms on how to meet with God. This week, we'll explore how to get the most out of those principles and rhythms. May God give you a true glimpse this week of the immeasurable glory and goodness he has in store for you every morning you set aside time to meet with him.

SCRIPTURE

"When the Spirit of truth comes, he will guide you into all the truth, for he will not speak on his own authority, but whatever he hears he will speak" (John 16:13).

DEVOTIONAL

God desires to speak directly to you. As a good Father, he longs to engage with you in continual conversation. So great was his longing for communication that he's given you the gift of the Holy Spirit. Because of Jesus' sacrifice and your decision to crown him Lord, you have access to the heart of God through the Spirit (Ephesians 1:13). You can know his will, hear his voice, and live with the knowledge of his love.

John 16:13 says, *"When the Spirit of truth comes, he will guide you into all the truth, for he will not speak on his own authority, but whatever he hears he will speak, and he will declare to you the things that are to come."* If you are a Christian, the *"Spirit of truth"* has come. He dwells within you. He longs to tell you how God feels about you. He longs to guide you to the Father's perfect, hopeful, and pleasing plans (Jeremiah 29:11). His voice is perfect, full of love, and always truthful. He will never guide you into something that isn't best for you. He will never speak hate or condemnation to you. As John 16:13 promises, he will declare to you what he hears the Father say.

Let the truth that God desires to have real, life-transforming conversations with you sink into your heart for a minute. Think about what it means for your life for you to have real communication with God. Your Creator longs to help you with your decisions, relationships, work, finances, and identity. God himself wants to talk with you about your life—to fully know you and be known by you.

> *Like any conversation, you will only hear him when you are listening.*

Just as any good parent loves talking with their children, your heavenly Father loves talking to you, his child. You see, God speaking to you is so little about your ability to hear his voice and so much more about his desire for you to know him. His voice in your life is just another product of grace, God's unmerited favor for those who believe. Like any conversation, you will only hear him when you are listening. And just like any good conversation, God longs to hear from you as well.

Hebrews 11:6 says, *"And without faith it is impossible to please him, for whoever would draw near to God must believe that he exists and that he rewards those who seek him."* Have faith that God longs to speak to you. Draw near to him in the assurance that he is already filled with love for you. The Holy Spirit longs to have a communicative relationship with you. Let the weight of conversation with God rest on his shoulders, trust in his word and his character, and listen to whatever he would speak to you today. He will speak to you because he wants to. The pressure isn't on you. This is a relationship, and the Holy Spirit is the perfect friend and guide.

Take time to quiet your heart and listen to the voice of the Spirit as we enter guided prayer today.

Notes:

GUIDED PRAYER

1. Take a moment to quiet your mind and soul. Reflect on John 16:13, that the words of Jesus would act as a foundation of truth and peace.

"When the Spirit of truth comes, he will guide you into all the truth, for he will not speak on his own authority, but whatever he hears he will speak, and he will declare to you the things that are to come" (John 16:13).

2. Now listen to God. If you have a situation, question, or anything you want to ask him, bring it before your Father in faith. God longs for you to tell him what you want help with. Even though he already knows your every need, the act of telling him your need makes this a conversation rather than unsolicited advice. Talk to God about your need and take note of any thoughts, feelings, words, or phrases that come to mind as his response.

"Behold, I stand at the door and knock. If anyone hears my voice and opens the door, I will come in to him and eat with him, and he with me" (Revelation 3:20).

3. Write down whatever God tells you. Don't be afraid to write, *"God said..."* Choosing to dwell in the reality that God speaks is foundational to living an abundant life in Jesus.

GO . . .

Communicating with God is similar to engaging in conversation with a close friend. I don't go to my friend and ask them to speak so I know they are real. Rather, I seek to know them as a person and conversation takes place as a result. Seek to know God as deeply as possible. Trust that he is real and that he speaks. Talk with him because you simply want to know him. And rest in the fact that conversation is a natural part of any healthy relationship. Your relationship with God is no different.

Soften Your Heart

WEEKLY OVERVIEW

Often, the biggest reason we struggle to meet with God consistently is that we don't know how to get the most out of our time alone with him. Last week in *Catalyst*, we learned some principles and rhythms on how to meet with God. This week, we'll explore how to get the most out of those principles and rhythms. May God give you a true glimpse this week of the immeasurable glory and goodness he has in store for you every morning you set aside time to meet with him.

SCRIPTURE

"As for what was sown on good soil, this is the one who hears the word and understands it. He indeed bears fruit and yields, in one case a hundredfold, in another sixty, and in another thirty" (Matthew 13:23)

DEVOTIONAL

One of the most important pursuits in getting the most out of our time alone with God is seeking to live with a soft heart.

In Matthew 13:22–23, Jesus teaches,

> *As for what was sown among thorns, this is the one who hears the word, but the cares of the world and the deceitfulness of riches choke the word, and it proves unfruitful. As for what was sown on good soil, this is the one who hears the word and understands it. He indeed bears fruit and yields, in one case a hundredfold, in another sixty, and in another thirty.*

The concept of good and bad soil is something Jesus' listeners would have understood well. Planting in good or bad soil meant having food or going hungry. It meant having money or living poor. For their agrarian culture, having good soil was a matter of survival.

> *Through our mindsets and postures of the heart, we can receive the seed of God's word, which will, in turn, yield life-giving fruit.*

While Jesus' parable might not have as direct of a correlation to us, its principle remains just as relevant. We all have spiritual soil. Through our mindsets and postures of the heart, we can receive the seed of God's word, which will, in turn, yield life-giving fruit. Or, we can allow the soil of our hearts to make us unreceptive to the powerful work of God in our lives.

It's incredibly important for us to understand that God never forces his desires on us. He waits patiently—beckoning us to open our hearts fully to him. He gently shows us his love, whispers his perfect plans to us, and waits for us to trust and surrender. With the grace of God, we can till the soil of our hearts, living receptively and surrendered to his loving-kindness and perfect will. If we cultivate a willing heart, God will mold and shape us into children free from the cares of the world and empowered to live Christ-like, fruitful lives.

Take time today to assess your life. What parts of your heart are hard to God? Where do you feel unreceptive to his goodness? Where do you need to say yes to God today in a fresh, transformative way?

In Ezekiel 36:26, God says, *"I will give you a new heart, and a new spirit I will put within you. And I will remove the heart of stone from your flesh and give you a heart of flesh."* Jesus paved the way for the soil of our hearts to be made soft, to be fashioned into his likeness. His Spirit dwells within you. He longs to work on your heart and guide you to a lifestyle of trust and surrender, that he might lead you to green pastures and still waters. May the Holy Spirit help you soften the soil of your heart today as you enter a time of guided prayer.

Notes:

GUIDED PRAYER

1. Take some time to receive God's presence. Open your heart to feel the peace and rest that comes from experiencing his nearness.

   "My presence will go with you, and I will give you rest" (Exodus 33:14).

2. Ask the Holy Spirit to reveal the parts of your heart that are hard toward him. Where is your life marked by striving rather than rest? In what situations are you struggling to bear the fruit of the Spirit? Where do you believe lies instead of truth? Decide on one area in which you would like to bear more fruit, to be more representative of the goodness of God.

   "But the fruit of the Spirit is love, joy, peace, patience, kindness, goodness, faithfulness, gentleness, self-control; against such things there is no law" (Galatians 5:22–23).

3. Bring that area to God. Engage in the work of making your heart softer by bringing it before God openly and honestly. Ask God to forgive your sin or correct the lie. Humble yourself before him and submit to his leadership rather than going about life on your own. Ask the Holy Spirit to work with you to soften your heart that you might bear his fruit in your life. Take whatever time you need to work on the soil of your heart with God in prayer.

   "If we confess our sins, he is faithful and just to forgive us our sins and to cleanse us from all unrighteousness" (1 John 1:9).

   "And I will give you a new heart, and a new spirit I will put within you. And I will remove the heart of stone from your flesh and give you a heart of flesh. And I will put my Spirit within you, and cause you to walk in my statutes and be careful to obey my rules" (Ezekiel 36:26–27).

GO . . .

Softening your heart is an important daily exercise. The more often you do it, the more you'll realize your need to have a soft heart. Having your heart fully open to God takes the mundane and makes it wonderful. It takes sunsets, conversations, prayers, work, and church and fills them with life, value, beauty, and joy. Take what you've learned today and continue to put it into practice. Choose to live a life positioned to receive the seed of God's wisdom, presence, and love that you might bear the fruit of the Spirit in every moment, every situation. May your day be marked by the fruit of the Spirit growing in new areas of your life, that his goodness would well up from new depths of communion and obedience.

Taste and See

WEEKLY OVERVIEW

Often, the biggest reason we struggle to meet with God consistently is that we don't know how to get the most out of our time alone with him. Last week in *Catalyst*, we learned some principles and rhythms on how to meet with God. This week, we'll explore how to get the most out of those principles and rhythms. May God give you a true glimpse this week of the immeasurable glory and goodness he has in store for you every morning you set aside time to meet with him.

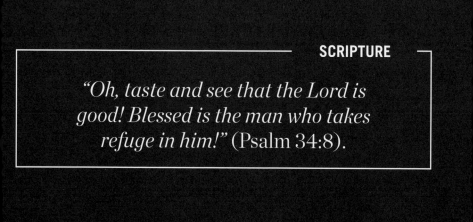

SCRIPTURE

"Oh, taste and see that the Lord is good! Blessed is the man who takes refuge in him!" (Psalm 34:8).

DEVOTIONAL

Psalm 34:8 is an amazing illustration of how foundational God's grace is to our seeking him. Scripture says, *"Oh, taste and see that the Lord is good! Blessed is the man who takes refuge in him!"* We believe as Christians that we need to take refuge in God. We believe that he is our source of provision, of life, and of all good things. But the barrier between our belief and our trust isn't trying harder; it's experiencing God's goodness.

God says, *"taste and see"* that I am good. He knows that when we experience his goodness, our hearts will naturally begin to trust him. He knows that when we experience his goodness, we will naturally begin to align our thoughts, emotions, and actions with the reality of his character, his love.

You and I are experiential beings. Studies have proven that decisions aren't actually made by logic; they're made by emotion. Even if you know logically that God is good, that he is worth your trust and your life, your moment-to-moment decisions won't line up with that logic unless you truly believe, on an emotional level, in God's goodness and trustworthiness. To trust God in every moment, you need fresh experiences with his goodness. To believe in his character over the lies the enemy lobs at you every day, you need to experience his character daily.

> ## *To trust God in every moment, you need fresh experiences with his goodness.*

The reality is, if you're having a difficult time trusting God or wanting to give your time and affection to him, the solution isn't to try harder but to simply stop and have a fresh experience with him. If you're having a hard time living free from a specific sin, freedom begins when you stop and experience the goodness of God's love and forgiveness and allow the reality of his love to draw you out of the world and into his loving embrace.

God longs to reveal his goodness to you today. He longs to show you all that he is doing to pursue you, provide for you, and draw you to himself. He longs to show you all the ways he's loving you. All that remains for your life to be marked by newfound fervor, freedom, and joy is for you to make space to *"taste and see"* how abundantly good your heavenly Father is. Out of experiencing God's goodness, allow your heart to be drawn into a lifestyle of trust and obedience.

Take time today in guided prayer to simply experience God's goodness. Choose to engage him not only with your mind but also your heart. And allow the reality of God's love to transform your life today.

Notes:

GUIDED PRAYER

1. Join your heart with David's as declared in Psalm 23:6. Allow Scripture to fill your heart with faith that you will experience God's goodness.

   "Surely goodness and mercy shall follow me all the days of my life, and I shall dwell in the house of the Lord forever" (Psalm 23:6).

2. Ask God for a revelation of how he's loving you right now. What is he doing around you, in your family, work, or heart? How is he revealing his goodness? Take a moment to reflect on his goodness at work in your life.

   "And we know that for those who love God all things work together for good, for those who are called according to his purpose" (Romans 8:28).

3. Thank God for his goodness. Reflect on all the ways he's revealing his love for you. Think about the good gifts you've been given. Allow the reality of God's goodness to stir up your heart to abide in him today.

   "I believe that I shall look upon the goodness of the Lord in the land of the living!" (Psalm 27:13).

GO . . .

Our effort in our relationship with God is far more about positioning ourselves to remember and experience God's goodness than drumming up desire or affection. If you don't feel like meeting with God, you're probably just in need of a fresh experience. So often, we learn to live dryly. We learn to live without abundant life, without the life-giving nature of God's presence. We settle for the fleeting satisfaction the world offers. But just a taste of God's goodness, just a moment of his presence, has the power to refresh our hearts and fill us with a yearning for that which we were made for: constant communion with our Creator. May you learn to *"taste and see"* that your God is good every day. And may your hunger for God ever increase as you discover how amazing life is when marked by the goodness of God's presence.

Trust

WEEKLY OVERVIEW

Often, the biggest reason we struggle to meet with God consistently is that we don't know how to get the most out of our time alone with him. Last week in *Catalyst*, we learned some principles and rhythms on how to meet with God. This week, we'll explore how to get the most out of those principles and rhythms. May God give you a true glimpse this week of the immeasurable glory and goodness he has in store for you every morning you set aside time to meet with him.

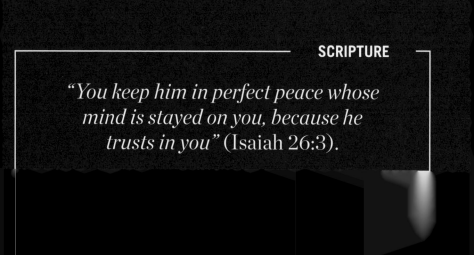

SCRIPTURE

"You keep him in perfect peace whose mind is stayed on you, because he trusts in you" (Isaiah 26:3).

Trust is the commodity of our heart with the highest value to God. Without trust, there can be no true relationship. Without trust, there is no moving forward. We are naturally so careful with whom we trust. One sign of a lie, one sign of wrong motivation, and we pull back. When we trust, we become vulnerable. When we trust, we expose our hearts, giving of ourselves. And when we trust in the wrong person, when our trust is broken, we get truly hurt.

Throughout the Old Testament, God proves himself to be entirely trustworthy. He repeatedly comes through for his people. After a phenomenal sign or miracle, the people have a season of trust. But then, time and time again, they doubt, pull back, and go their own way. They stop trusting God and trust in that which they can see, that which they can control.

> *Without trust, we're stuck measuring the value of God's commands, leadership, and love.*

Often, we're no different from them. God has always been faithful to me. The truth that he works all things for my good has been proven over and over again in my life (Romans 8:28). But when things get hard, or when the world tempts me to become self-sufficient, I pull back my trust and go my own way.

Foundational to experiencing all that God has for us is giving him our trust. Without trust, our relationship with him becomes transactional. Without trust, we're stuck measuring the value of God's commands, leadership, and love. To experience fullness of life in our time alone with God, to follow our Good Shepherd to green pastures and still waters, and to receive every good gift he longs to give us, we must come to a place of trust.

So, where are you trusting yourself above God? What command has he given you that you haven't been obedient to yet? In what ways are you striving in your own strength instead of abiding in the reality of God's power and faithfulness? What wounds are you holding back from his healing out of fear or pain?

Take time today to meet with your heavenly Father. Remind yourself of his trustworthiness. Take a step forward in giving him more of your heart. And experience the peace and fruit that comes from following his command to trust and obey.

Notes:

GUIDED PRAYER

1. Meditate on God's word. Allow his character to soften your heart and empower you to trust.

   "If we are faithless, he remains faithful – for he cannot deny himself" (2 Timothy 2:13).

   "For the word of the Lord is upright, and all his work is done in faithfulness" (Psalm 33:4).

   "Trust in the Lord, and do good; dwell in the land and befriend faithfulness. Delight yourself in the Lord, and he will give you the desires of your heart. Commit your way to the Lord; trust in him, and he will act" (Psalm 37:3–5).

2. Identify one area in which you're having a hard time trusting God. Look for where you are striving in life. Look for what causes you the most stress.

3. Ask the Holy Spirit for a pathway to trusting God more. Why is it that you have a hard time trusting God? What will it take for you to trust God wholeheartedly? Take some time to journal and ask God to empower you to trust him. Give him your trust and receive his peace in return.

   "You keep him in perfect peace whose mind is stayed on you, because he trusts in you. Trust in the Lord forever, for the Lord God is an everlasting rock" (Isaiah 26:3–4).

   "Trust in the Lord with all your heart, and do not lean on your own understanding. In all your ways acknowledge him, and he will make straight your paths. Be not wise in your own eyes; fear the Lord, and turn away from evil. It will be healing to your flesh and refreshment to your bones" (Proverbs 3:5–8).

GO . . .

There is no substitute for true trust. You can't fake your way into the promises of God. You can't act your way into fullness of relationship. The difficult work of looking at our hearts and allowing God to move in healing, of being transparent and honest every day, is the only pathway to all God has for us. That's why spending time alone with God is so vital to every other part of life. Without looking at our hearts every day and identifying places that need to be transformed by God's power and love, we'll be like the Israelites and go our own way into chaos and destruction. God wants to remind you of his love every morning. He wants to root and ground you in the reality of his faithfulness that you might trust him at every turn in your day. Devote yourself to the rhythm of meeting with God every morning and watch as the entirety of your day changes for the better.

Obedience

WEEKLY OVERVIEW

Often, the biggest reason we struggle to meet with God consistently is that we don't know how to get the most out of our time alone with him. Last week in *Catalyst*, we learned some principles and rhythms on how to meet with God. This week, we'll explore how to get the most out of those principles and rhythms. May God give you a true glimpse this week of the immeasurable glory and goodness he has in store for you every morning you set aside time to meet with him.

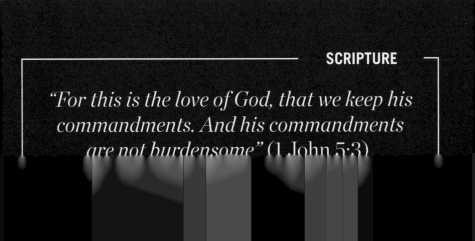

SCRIPTURE

"For this is the love of God, that we keep his commandments. And his commandments are not burdensome" (1 John 5:3)

DEVOTIONAL

Throughout our lives, we are commanded to obey. Whether it's a parent telling us "Pick that up," or "Don't do that," or a government laying down a law, we acknowledge obedience as a necessary part of life. And so often, because we grow up with some sense of the purpose of obedience, we apply our worldly notions of obedience to our relationship with God. We see the commands of Scripture or feel a prompting from the Spirit and sense a similar tone of command.

The problem with carrying a worldly notion of obedience into our relationship with God is that no one, no matter how loving, can or will fully care for us the way our heavenly Father does. No matter how good the lawmaker, parent, friend, or teacher is, no one truly loves us like God does.

Isaiah 1:19 promises us, *"If you are willing and obedient, you shall eat the good of the land."* God asks for us to be obedient to him because his plan is always for our betterment. He sees what lies ahead of us. He knows the potential perils or consequences of our actions. And as a Good Shepherd, he longs to guide us into an incredibly abundant life filled with all the goodness of his kingdom.

> *No one, no matter how loving, can or will fully care for us the way our heavenly Father does.*

If we are ever going to experience the wealth of glorious inheritance God has for us, we must learn to trust him and obey. God can't lead us to still waters and plentiful pastures if we are unwilling to follow him. He can't lead us into the depths of his love if we don't trust in his loving-kindness. He can't lead us into consistent encounters with him if we don't trust that he is as near as his word promises. And he can't satisfy the deep desires of our hearts if we don't trust that his purposes for us will truly satiate our longings.

First Samuel 15:22 says, *"Has the Lord as great delight in burnt offerings and sacrifices, as in obeying the voice of the Lord? Behold, to obey is better than sacrifice, and to listen than the fat of rams."* God longs to fashion us into children who are quick to obey him, that we would quickly experience the good fruit of his wisdom and guidance. He earnestly desires our obedience because he earnestly desires abundant life for us that only comes through acting upon his thoughts and his ways.

Take time in guided prayer to reflect on the importance of obedience to God's commands. Think about the times that obeying his commands would have been better than a choice you made outside of his direction. Think about a time that you obeyed him and that decision bore good fruit in your life. May today's time of guided prayer lead you to a fruitful lifestyle of immediate obedience to your good and loving Father.

Notes:

GUIDED PRAYER

1. Meditate on the importance of obedience. Allow Scripture to fill you with a desire to obey God sooner and to greater measures.

   "Why do you call me 'Lord, Lord,' and not do what I tell you?" (Luke 6:46).

   "If you are willing and obedient, you shall eat the good of the land" (Isaiah 1:19).

   "Has the Lord as great delight in burnt offerings and sacrifices, as in obeying the voice of the Lord? Behold, to obey is better than sacrifice, and to listen than the fat of rams" (1 Samuel 15:22).

2. Why do you have a hard time obeying God's word or his promptings? What's one specific area in which you have a hard time obeying God?

3. Reflect on his promises in that area and place your trust in him. Ask God for a revelation of the good things he has in store for you if you obey. Allow God's goodness to empower you to live a lifestyle of immediate obedience.

   "This Book of the Law shall not depart from your mouth, but you shall meditate on it day and night, so that you may be careful to do according to all that is written in it. For then you will make your way prosperous, and then you will have good success" (Joshua 1:8).

   "Every good gift and every perfect gift is from above, coming down from the Father of lights, with whom there is no variation or shadow due to change" (James 1:17).

   "For you know the grace of our Lord Jesus Christ, that though he was rich, yet for your sake he became poor, so that you by his poverty might become rich" (2 Corinthians 8:9).

GO . . .

Placing our trust in someone is always a process. God does not assume that you will fully trust him until you truly get to know him. To know his love and kindness in a way that will result in trust takes time spent daily developing your relationship. If you want to experience the fruit of obedience and trust, you must make time to get to know your heavenly Father. In a moment where you feel like going your own way, you must have a solid foundation built on knowing the goodness of God and his word. Have patience with yourself, and center your life around developing a greater relationship with your heavenly Father. May you come to know the heart of God as described in Ephesians 3:17–19:

> *That you, being rooted and grounded in love, may have strength to comprehend with all the saints what is the breadth and length and height and depth, and to know the love of Christ that surpasses knowledge, that you may be filled with all the fullness of God.*

WEEK

Foundation

FOUR

Value Your Foundation

WEEKLY OVERVIEW

In the final week of *Catalyst*, we'll lay a foundation stone each day for a healthy, life-giving time alone with God that you might be equipped to flourish in your relationship with God in and out of every season. May you be rooted and grounded in the unshakable love and grace of God this week. May the availability of God's presence and the power of experiencing his love become the solid rock on which you stand. And may God build a foundation in your heart on which you can stand firmly and securely in him, no matter what life brings your way.

SCRIPTURE

"He only is my rock and my salvation, my fortress; I shall not be shaken" (Psalm 62:6).

DEVOTIONAL

All of us have a foundation we're living on day to day. Some days, our foundation might be ourselves. We trust in our perception and beliefs and live and work following the notion that we know best. Other days, our foundation is the opinion of others. We live and work to earn the affection of those around us. Our foundation is always in fluid motion as the perceptions and ideals of others around us inevitably change. For the days we live on the foundation of God, on his unchanging will and perfect desires, our foundation is the solid rock of God's unshakable character and unending love.

I spend too little time assessing the foundation I'm living on from day to day. It's so easy to jump out of bed and straight into the world. When I live that way, my life is typically a response to what's right around me instead of a conscious choice. My day feels like I'm constantly playing catch-up rather than living intentionally. I make decisions, feel, and think in response to the ever-shifting world around me instead of living based on the presence and principles of my heavenly Father.

> *I need the foundation of God's presence and principles to experience the wonders of living in God's kingdom, of living on earth as it is in heaven.*

I might be able to live that way for a while. But living apart from the foundation of God's character and love is exhausting. The world will always fail me, and the wisdom of man is folly, whether it's my own or someone else's. I need the foundation of God's presence and principles to experience the wonders of living in God's kingdom, of living on earth as it is in heaven.

To do that, I need a fresh experience with God, with the Creator of heaven and earth, every day.

The first stone to lay in building a firm foundation is deciding to value your foundation at all. If you take time to think about the value of being rooted and grounded in the love and nearness of your heavenly Father, you'll have the encouragement you need to establish a firm foundation. If you humble yourself in acknowledgment that only God is wise, only God knows best, it will go a long way toward leading you to a lifestyle of abiding in God, that your life might be filled with his fruit.

Take time today in guided prayer to assess your foundation. Ask yourself, what is guiding you? What is motivating you? Why are you living the way you are? May God illuminate your heart today as you pray. And may he become the firm foundation on which you experience the fullness of his promises.

Notes:

GUIDED PRAYER

1. What foundation are you living from? What is guiding your decisions, emotions, and actions? What's your motivation? Take a moment to reflect and journal.

2. Meditate on God's desire to be your foundation. Think about what your life would look like if you were firmly established every day in the character and reality of your heavenly Father.

   "Behold, I am the one who has laid as a foundation in Zion, a stone, a tested stone, a precious cornerstone, of a sure foundation: 'Whoever believes will not be in haste'" (Isaiah 28:16).

   "Everyone then who hears these words of mine and does them will be like a wise man who built his house on the rock" (Matthew 7:24).

   "In him we live and move and have our being" (Acts 17:28).

3. What would it take for you to live from the foundation of God's word and presence? What's in the way of that right now? What do you need to do more of? What do you need to do less of? Ask God to show you one step you can take today to establish him as your foundation.

GO . . .

One of the most important parts of establishing a firm foundation in God is spending time in his word. His word never changes. God has already spoken his truth on so many of life's matters. But to live in obedience to God's word, we first have to read it, and, second, we have to allow it time to move from our head to our heart. We must allow God's word to become the foundation on which we make decisions. We must allow it to shape the lens through which we see the world. May the word of God spoken to you lead you to transcendent peace and unshakable faith. And may your foundation become more and more secure as you spend time every day in God's presence, establishing yourself in the reality of his kingdom.

Set Your Values

WEEKLY OVERVIEW

In the final week of *Catalyst*, we'll lay a foundation stone each day for a
healthy, life-giving time alone with God that you might be equipped to
flourish in your relationship with God in and out of every season. May you
be rooted and grounded in the unshakable love and grace of God this week.
May the availability of God's presence and the power of experiencing his love
become the solid rock on which you stand. And may God build a foundation
in your heart on which you can stand firmly and securely in him, no matter
what life brings your way.

SCRIPTURE

*"But seek first the kingdom of God and
his righteousness, and all these things
will be added to you"* (Matthew 6:33).

DEVOTIONAL

The depth of your relationship with God will always be predicated on where you've set your values. You spend time on those things you value most. You spend time with the people you value most. Our value system is in many ways the entire foundation on which we think, feel, and act.

It's for this reason Jesus says in Matthew 6:33, *"But seek first the kingdom of God and his righteousness, and all these things will be added to you."* The Message translation says it this way:

> *Steep your life in God-reality, God-initiative, God-provisions. Don't worry about missing out. You'll find all your everyday human concerns will be met.*

When we value God and his kingdom first, we'll find that he has already looked after every core need and desire in our hearts. He loves to provide for both our needs and wants as our hearts grow in alignment with his (Psalm 37:4). He's a good Father who loves to see his children thrive. He's a God of limitless resources who provides for us perfectly, leading to true satisfaction in our body and soul.

> *When we value God and his kingdom first, we'll find that he has already looked after every core need and desire in our hearts.*

But foundational to receiving all that God longs to give is valuing him first. He longs to give you peace and joy every single morning, that he would be your safe refuge all day, no matter what the world throws at you. But to receive that heavenly gift, you must value God enough to make time for him in the morning. The Holy Spirit longs to lead you to righteous living. He wants to reveal the intent behind God's commandments as you open God's word, and he wants to lead you away from temptation every moment of the day. But you must value his leadership and his word above the temptation of the world to experience the wonders of righteous living.

There are countless examples of the blessings and benefits of walking with God. So, take time today in guided prayer to assess your value system, and decide to value God and his kingdom above all else. Surrender before him any ways of thinking or acting that aren't in line with his character and his kingdom. And lay a firm foundation of steeping your life daily in *"God-reality, God-initiative, [and] God-provisions."*

Notes:

GUIDED PRAYER

1. What do you consistently value most? Maybe it's the opinion of others. Maybe it's a sense of security. Maybe it's your own desires, your own opinion. Ask the Holy Spirit to illuminate your heart, and come before God openly and honestly with what you find together.

   "Search me, O God, and know my heart! Try me and know my thoughts! And see if there be any grievous way in me, and lead me in the way everlasting!" (Psalm 139:23–24).

2. Surrender to God anything you've valued above him and receive his peace and forgiveness. Take a moment to simply rest in the goodness of God's presence.

   "The Lord is good to those who wait for him, to the soul who seeks him" (Lamentations 3:25).

3. Choose to value God above all else. Decide to make space for him first. Decide to follow his wisdom and leadership above yours or the world's. And receive the peace that comes from choosing to be a faithful sheep to the one Good Shepherd.

   "Steep your life in God-reality, God-initiative, God-provisions. Don't worry about missing out. You'll find all your everyday human concerns will be met" (Matthew 6:33 MSG).

   "The Lord is my shepherd; I shall not want. He makes me lie down in green pastures. He leads me beside still waters. He restores my soul. He leads me in paths of righteousness for his name's sake" (Psalm 23:1–3).

GO . . .

Valuing God above all else is a daily exercise. But the more you do it, the more natural it will become. After choosing to follow his wisdom and leadership day in and day out, it begins to feel more natural than following the world or going your own way. After meeting with God every morning for a while and experiencing the wonders of starting your day by receiving his unconditional love, it will feel strange to go about your day without that time. God longs to give you a new normal. He has the power to change anything and everything that's holding you back from the fullness of life he died to bring you. May steeping your life in all God is become your new normal as you seek him first.

Because You Matter

WEEKLY OVERVIEW

In the final week of *Catalyst*, we'll lay a foundation stone each day for a healthy, life-giving time alone with God that you might be equipped to flourish in your relationship with God in and out of every season. May you be rooted and grounded in the unshakable love and grace of God this week. May the availability of God's presence and the power of experiencing his love become the solid rock on which you stand. And may God build a foundation in your heart on which you can stand firmly and securely in him, no matter what life brings your way.

SCRIPTURE

"Are not five sparrows sold for two pennies? And not one of them is forgotten before God. Why, even the hairs of your head are all numbered. Fear not; you are of more value than many sparrows" (Luke 12:6–7).

For most of my life, I felt that believing I was valuable was prideful. I thought that to live humbly, I had to have low self-worth. I thought that fighting for a good life, for a life marked by abundance, was selfish. But, early on in developing the rhythm of spending time alone with God, I discovered something surprising and life-changing: I am God's most prized possession.

I remember it so clearly. I was reflecting on the cross, visualizing the sacrifice Christ made for me. In a moment of true honesty, of heartfelt worship, the words *Thank you, God* rose from the bottom of my heart. In response, clear as day, God spoke to my heart, "You were worth it." I was completely taken aback. The sense God gave me at that moment is that even if Jesus' sacrifice was just for my salvation, even if I were the only one who came to believe, that I would have been worth it to him. So great is God's love for me, so deep was his longing to have a restored relationship with me, that he sent his only Son, for me. At that moment, I realized how much my life matters. In the days that have followed, God has only ever shown me in more ways how deeply he cares about me. Luke 15:8–10 says:

> *What woman, having ten silver coins, if she loses one coin, does not light a lamp and sweep the house and seek diligently until she finds it? And when she has found it, she calls together her friends and neighbors, saying, "Rejoice with me, for I have found the coin that I had lost." Just so, I tell you, there is joy before the angels of God over one sinner who repents.*

> *You are God's most prized possession. He cares deeply about you. He's not just God of a group of people; he is your God.*

You are God's most prized possession. He cares deeply about you. He's not just God of a group of people; he is your God. He had you, specifically you, in his heart when he sent his Son to die. You are worth the death of Jesus.

Understanding your value to God is foundational to living the life Jesus died to give you. If you have a low value of yourself, you'll settle for less than God intends for you. But if you begin to live from the revelation of your value to God, you won't settle for sin any longer, and you won't settle for the opinion of man. You won't live like you're lower than other people or unworthy of love. You won't waste your life on frivolous pursuits that don't truly satisfy your heart. Instead, you'll settle for nothing less than the fullness of life, of love, of purpose that Jesus died to give you.

Take time today to receive a revelation of your value to God. Allow the Holy Spirit to convict you of any ways you're not living in line with your value. And surrender to God every part of your life that's not befitting of one so deeply loved, so deeply cared for, by such a good Father.

Notes:

GUIDED PRAYER

1. Meditate on how much God loves you that he would send his only Son to die for you. May the Holy Spirit give you a tangible revelation of God's love at this moment.

   "But God, being rich in mercy, because of the great love with which he loved us, even when we were dead in our trespasses, made us alive together with Christ—by grace you have been saved—and raised us up with him and seated us with him in the heavenly places in Christ Jesus, so that in the coming ages he might show the immeasurable riches of his grace in kindness toward us in Christ Jesus" (Ephesians 2:4–7).

   "For God so loved the world, that he gave his only Son, that whoever believes in him should not perish but have eternal life" (John 3:16).

2. What in your life doesn't align with how valuable you are? What do you believe about yourself that God doesn't believe? What are you doing that's not congruent with someone who is a child of God? Where are you not enjoying the fruit of being so deeply loved by the Creator and Lord of all?

   "Consider the ravens: they neither sow nor reap, they have neither storehouse nor barn, and yet God feeds them. Of how much more value are you than the birds!" (Luke 12:24).

   "See what kind of love the Father has given to us, that we should be called children of God; and so we are" (1 John 3:1).

3. Surrender before your loving Father any lie, any lifestyle, any wrong mindset that's keeping you from experiencing all Jesus died to give you. Choose to receive and believe the value that God has for you. Cast aside any lies the world has spoken over you and beliefs birthed from failure or wounds, and choose to believe that God is the only one who sees you correctly, perfectly.

He heals the brokenhearted and binds up their wounds (Psalm 147:3).

"For I will restore health to you, and your wounds I will heal, declares the Lord, because they have called you an outcast: 'It is Zion, for whom no one cares!'" (Jeremiah 30:17).

"Bless the Lord, O my soul, and forget not all his benefits, who forgives all your iniquity, who heals all your diseases, who redeems your life from the pit, who crowns you with steadfast love and mercy" (Psalm 103:2–4).

GO . . .

Know that God has the power to take anything you surrender and move in healing and in truth. You can live differently today. You can be set free today. Nothing stands in the way of you living a better life when God is on your side. He is for you. He is your provider, your giver of every good gift. Come before him today with belief in your heart that things can be different, and follow your Good Shepherd to green pastures and still waters.

Live in Today

WEEKLY OVERVIEW

In the final week of *Catalyst*, we'll lay a foundation stone each day for a healthy, life-giving time alone with God that you might be equipped to flourish in your relationship with God in and out of every season. May you be rooted and grounded in the unshakable love and grace of God this week. May the availability of God's presence and the power of experiencing his love become the solid rock on which you stand. And may God build a foundation in your heart on which you can stand firmly and securely in him, no matter what life brings your way.

SCRIPTURE

"Therefore do not be anxious about tomorrow, for tomorrow will be anxious for itself. Sufficient for the day is its own trouble" (Matthew 6:34).

DEVOTIONAL

A cornerstone of experiencing consistent, transcendent peace is choosing to be present, to live in today. While God dwells in eternity, we only dwell in the here and now. And God only speaks, provides, blesses, anoints, and fills us up in the here and now. To abide in God is to abide moment to moment. To bear the fruit of the Spirit is to commune with him in the present. To hear from God and follow his leadership is to follow him one step at a time, one day at a time.

God never promises his presence or provision for tomorrow. In fact, Scripture is clear that our focus is always to be on today and that we are called to a lifestyle of trust. In response to people's fear about God's continued provision, Jesus commands in Matthew 6:34, *"Do not be anxious about tomorrow, for tomorrow will be anxious for itself. Sufficient for the day is its own trouble."*

> *Spending time worrying about tomorrow only robs us of all the goodness to experience today.*

Perhaps the best picture of this is God's people wandering in the desert. The Lord provided enough manna for every individual day except for the day before the Sabbath, where the people were permitted to collect enough for two days. And God led his people by a pillar of fire or cloud to where they were to go next and never farther.

God doesn't lead and provide this way out of spite. There is nothing to enjoy about tomorrow. There is no goodness in tomorrow. Spending time worrying about tomorrow only robs us of all the goodness to experience today. Spending time dwelling on what could be keeps from enjoying what is. There is no wisdom in worry. Planning apart from the leadership of God is folly.

Only he knows what opportunities will present themselves. Only he knows what trials will come. And his preparation for both lies in giving ourselves fully to this moment.

To experience the fullness of life God longs to give you, you must make the choice every moment to trust God with your future and enjoy that which he's given you today. Be faithful to the work he has already put before you. Love those who are already around you. Enjoy the gifts he's already given you. And let every other concern, every other fear, every other question go. God says, *"Therefore do not be anxious, saying, 'What shall we eat?' or 'What shall we drink?' or 'What shall we wear?' For the Gentiles seek after all these things, and your heavenly Father knows that you need them all. But seek first the kingdom of God and his righteousness, and all these things will be added to you"* (Matthew 6:31–33).

As we enter a time of guided prayer, may the promise of God's continued faithfulness fill you with courage to live in today. And may you experience a profound sense of peace and fullness of life as you seek to grab hold of all that God has for you at this moment, here and now.

Notes:

GUIDED PRAYER

1. Reflect on God's command to live in the here and now. May the Holy Spirit illuminate why God would have you live this way as you meditate on his word.

"Do not be anxious, saying, 'What shall we eat?' or 'What shall we drink?' or 'What shall we wear?' For the Gentiles seek after all these things, and your heavenly Father knows that you need them all. But seek first the kingdom of God and his righteousness, and all these things will be added to you. Therefore do not be anxious about tomorrow, for tomorrow will be anxious for itself. Sufficient for the day is its own trouble" (Matthew 6:31–34).

2. What causes you the most fear over the future? What belief or stress of life draws you out of enjoying the moment?

3. Take time and give that belief or stress over to God. Ask God for the courage to trust him with it. As you surrender, take hold of the peace that comes from trusting in your good and faithful Father here and now, acknowledging that he holds every moment, past, present, and future, in his hands.

"Come to me, all who labor and are heavy laden, and I will give you rest. Take my yoke upon you, and learn from me, for I am gentle and lowly in heart, and you will find rest for your souls. For my yoke is easy, and my burden is light" (Matthew 11:28–30).

GO . . .

Fighting to live in the moment is a daily battle. You have an enemy who would love nothing more than to cause you to live in constant fear. Trusting God that he will provide for every part of your life is uncommon even among believers. But know that just as God did with Joseph, your heavenly Father will prepare you if a famine is to come. And just as God did with David, he will provide the pathway to victory over every enemy when they attack. As you seek first God and his kingdom, he will direct your thoughts and actions that you might receive every good thing he longs to give you. Choose to live in today, in this moment, and grab hold of all the goodness God is giving you right now. Take in the beauty of what's around you. Enjoy the people in your life. And experience what it's like to be a beloved sheep in the well-guarded, perfectly provided-for flock of your Good Shepherd.

The Importance of Peace

WEEKLY OVERVIEW

In the final week of *Catalyst*, we'll lay a foundation stone each day for a healthy, life-giving time alone with God that you might be equipped to flourish in your relationship with God in and out of every season. May you be rooted and grounded in the unshakable love and grace of God this week. May the availability of God's presence and the power of experiencing his love become the solid rock on which you stand. And may God build a foundation in your heart on which you can stand firmly and securely in him, no matter what life brings your way.

SCRIPTURE

"Now may the Lord of peace himself give you peace at all times in every way" (2 Thessalonians 3:16).

DEVOTIONAL

Most of the time, I view peace as a luxury. Peace is that thing you feel when you have a break in between the important stuff. It comes and goes, and that's just life. Sometimes the feeling of peace even makes me nervous, like I'm forgetting something. Peace is one of the many costs of success, of working hard enough, or of caring enough.

But when I look at Scripture and sense God's heart as I meet with him, I find that he really cares about peace. I'm discovering that, to God, peace isn't a luxury; it's a support beam on which the Christian life is meant to be built. Philippians 4:6–7 says:

> *Do not be anxious about anything, but in everything by prayer and supplication with thanksgiving let your requests be made known to God. And the peace of God, which surpasses all understanding, will guard your hearts and your minds in Christ Jesus.*

> ### *It's far easier to be led by the Spirit, to love others well, and to resist temptation when I'm at peace in my heart and mind.*

God longs for our peace not to be based on our circumstances or understanding but on his goodness and faithfulness. He longs for us to so trust him, that when we cast our anxieties on him, we would exchange our worries for his peace.

Every morning as I meet with God, he seeks to fill my heart with peace. He illuminates those things that are keeping me from experiencing the fruit of the Spirit and guides me to a lifestyle of surrender, that I would receive the incredible gift of transcendent peace. As I commit myself to experiencing all he has for me, I've been discovering something incredible: I am only my true self when I'm at peace. Peace brings out the best of me, the true identity I've been given by God.

I'm learning that it's far easier to be led by the Spirit, to love others well, and to resist temptation when I'm at peace in my heart and mind. Fear, insecurity, and worry are at odds with the work God is doing in my life. They're at odds with the truth that God really is good, really is present, and really is for me. Peace isn't a luxury to life in God; it's a necessity.

Take time today to reflect on the importance of peace. Allow the Lord to illuminate the people, circumstances, or lies that are most robbing you of peace. And exchange your fear, stress, doubt, and worry for the transcendent peace of your good Father.

Notes:

GUIDED PRAYER

1. Meditate on God's process and promise of peace. May the words of Scripture stir your heart to fight for what's yours in God.

   "Do not be anxious about anything, but in everything by prayer and supplication with thanksgiving let your requests be made known to God. And the peace of God, which surpasses all understanding, will guard your hearts and your minds in Christ Jesus" (Philippians 4:6–7).

   "Now may the Lord of peace himself give you peace at all times in every way" (2 Thessalonians 3:16).

   "But the fruit of the Spirit is love, joy, peace, patience, kindness, goodness, faithfulness, gentleness, self-control; against such things there is no law" (Galatians 5:22–23).

2. Think about the times you are most without peace. How do you feel? How do you act? Ask the Holy Spirit to illuminate a root issue that's robbing you of peace. Take a moment and compare that issue with God's truth.

   "I sought the Lord, and he answered me and delivered me from all my fears" (Psalm 34:4).

3. Ask God for his plan to redeem and restore that root cause. Maybe you need to trust more. Maybe you need to concern yourself more with how God feels about you than how you perceive others feel about you. Ask God for his solution, and commit yourself to working with him until you're experiencing consistent peace.

   "For to set the mind on the flesh is death, but to set the mind on the Spirit is life and peace" (Romans 8:6).

   "Turn away from evil and do good; seek peace and pursue it" (Psalm 34:14).

GO . . .

The reality is that we will never live perfectly. There will always be moments that we allow the world to get the better of us. But what matters is what we do in those moments. Will we fight for the peace that God longs to give us? Will we believe that his peace is available in every moment, in every circumstance? Or will we believe the world, that peace really is just a luxury? Your experience in this life is all about what you fight to believe of God and receive from God. May God fill you with the courage and belief to fight for peace in all circumstances, to his glory and your good.

Have Grace for Yourself

WEEKLY OVERVIEW

In the final week of *Catalyst*, we'll lay a foundation stone each day for a healthy, life-giving time alone with God that you might be equipped to flourish in your relationship with God in and out of every season. May you be rooted and grounded in the unshakable love and grace of God this week. May the availability of God's presence and the power of experiencing his love become the solid rock on which you stand. And may God build a foundation in your heart on which you can stand firmly and securely in him, no matter what life brings your way.

SCRIPTURE

"As a father shows compassion to his children, so the Lord shows compassion to those who fear him. For he knows our frame; he remembers that we are dust" (Psalm 103:13–14).

DEVOTIONAL

Perhaps the most counterintuitive aspect of spiritual growth is the importance of having grace for yourself. Whenever I sin, miss a morning of time alone with God, or treat someone poorly, I always tend to beat myself up. I'm continually surprised by my imperfection. I have less grace for myself than God does. And instead of allowing God to build me up after a mistake, I tend to tear myself down even more.

> *When we stop demanding perfection and start seeing ourselves as God sees us, we'll allow him to be strong in our weakness.*

Psalm 103:13–14 says, *"As a father shows compassion to his children, so the Lord shows compassion to those who fear him. For he knows our frame; he remembers that we are dust."* God knows that we're imperfect. He knows that we'll never love him or others as well as we hope. He knows that we'll never fully be without sin in this life. And he knows that the best way to propel us forward, to grow and develop us, is to offer us grace upon grace.

A key to enjoying this life God has given us is being quick to forgive ourselves. When we stop demanding perfection and start seeing ourselves as God sees us, we'll allow him to be strong in our weakness. Mistakes and sins become opportunities for God to reveal the depths of his love when we allow ourselves to be forgiven and restored to right relationship with him. Our imperfections become opportunities to see God's grace at work in real time when we allow him to correct and redeem our wrongdoings. In this way, mistakes become opportunities for experiencing God's growth in us.

Psalm 103:8 says, *"The Lord is merciful and gracious, slow to anger and abounding in steadfast love."* God's plan to propel you forward, to fashion you into the likeness of Jesus, is paved by grace and forgiveness. There is no place for self-deprecation in our journey with God. So, allow the Lord to show compassion to you today. Lift up your eyes and see the warmth and love in his face. Allow his steadfast love to carry you through the victories and failures that are to come. Choose grace for yourself, that you would see yourself as God does and experience life in his love.

Take time in guided prayer to discover lies and wounds that haven't been touched by the healing hands of your loving Father. Allow the Holy Spirit to lift your eyes that you might see God for who he is, and choose to have grace for yourself as he does.

Notes:

GUIDED PRAYER

1. Reflect on the nature of your imperfection. Ask God for his wisdom and perspective.

    "As a father shows compassion to his children, so the Lord shows compassion to those who fear him. For he knows our frame; he remembers that we are dust" (Psalm 103:13–14).

    "If we say we have no sin, we deceive ourselves, and the truth is not in us. If we confess our sins, he is faithful and just to forgive us our sins and to cleanse us from all unrighteousness" (1 John 1:8–9).

2. Where do you need God's grace today? What mistake, sin, or wound needs the healing touch of God's forgiveness and love? Bring it before God today, trusting that his hands are strong but gentle and his heart is filled with love for you.

    "The Lord your God is in your midst, a mighty one who will save; he will rejoice over you with gladness; he will quiet you by his love; he will exult over you with loud singing" (Zephaniah 3:17).

    "For we do not have a high priest who is unable to sympathize with our weaknesses, but one who in every respect has been tempted as we are, yet without sin" (Hebrews 4:15).

3. Take time to rest in God's forgiveness and grace. Allow his love to restore you to joy and abundant life. Choose today to leave behind your mistakes, and live in light of God's present grace.

    "Let us then with confidence draw near to the throne of grace, that we may receive mercy and find grace to help in time of need" (Hebrews 4:16).

GO . . .

Foundational to forgiving others is learning to forgive yourself. When you become someone who has grace for yourself, you'll better be able to extend grace to others. Life is so much richer when we remove the expectation of perfection and live on the foundation of God's continual grace. May you experience the peace and joy that comes from receiving grace upon grace from your good and loving Father. And may his goodness and love lead you to an abundant life marked by God building you up rather than continually tearing yourself down.

You Can Do It

WEEKLY OVERVIEW

In the final week of *Catalyst*, we'll lay a foundation stone each day for a healthy, life-giving time alone with God that you might be equipped to flourish in your relationship with God in and out of every season. May you be rooted and grounded in the unshakable love and grace of God this week. May the availability of God's presence and the power of experiencing his love become the solid rock on which you stand. And may God build a foundation in your heart on which you can stand firmly and securely in him, no matter what life brings your way.

SCRIPTURE

"I can do all things through him who strengthens me" (Philippians 4:13).

DEVOTIONAL

One of the most challenging decisions God asks us to make is to line up our belief in ourselves with the truth of his perspective. Every day, every moment, we either trust in God or ourselves. Every new morning is an opportunity to believe that we truly *"can do all things through him who strengthens [us]"* or to live pretty much like we did the day before and all the days before that. Change is difficult. It requires stepping out into the unknown with belief in our hearts that we can rise to unknown occasions, take hold of new opportunities, face challenges we've never met before, and, in God, come out victorious.

> *Foundational to spending time alone with God is believing in yourself, not because of your own strength, but because you are the child of a good Father with perfect perspective who believes in you.*

Foundational to spending time alone with God is believing in yourself, not because of your own strength, but because you are the child of a good Father with perfect perspective who believes in you. It's not easy to wake up early. It's not easy to carve out time in your busy schedule. It's not easy to say no to entertainment, to friends, to whatever is competing for time spent alone in God's presence. But you can do it. There's no one to stop you but yourself.

Our lives are built by thousands of momentary decisions. On average, our lives are about 27,000 days long. We won't remember most of those days. We won't remember how we felt or how we spent our time. But the entirety of our lives here on earth is comprised of decisions that seemed minor at the moment but, when strung together, define us.

Every morning, you're faced with a decision. Are you going to make space to meet with your Creator, be rooted and grounded in his love, and be equipped to better abide with him throughout your day? Or are you going to rush out into the day before you and most likely live from the same habits and rituals as the day before? Foundational to that decision is either belief or doubt. You will either believe that you can change, you can make better decisions, and you can choose God and the amazing life he has for you. Or you will doubt yourself and his power in your life to lead you to something more.

Hear today that you can do it. If I can do it, if thousands of believers around the world can do it, you can do it. You can experience God's loving presence every morning. You can hear his voice. You can bear the fruit of the Spirit. You can be changed. You can be used by God to change others. Every promise, every word from God's mouth to his people, is meant for you. Take hold of those promises today. Allow the Holy Spirit to stir up belief in your heart. Decide today that you can do this. And rest in the knowledge that you'll never go it alone. You have a loving, present Father filled with grace and power there to help you every step of the way.

Notes:

GUIDED PRAYER

1. Reflect for a moment on the value of meeting with God every day. Reflect on experiences you've had with God across the last 28 days. How did your decision to go deeper with God, to experience his presence, affect your life for the better?

2. What steps do you need to take to carve out space to meet with God every day? What would it take to be honest, worship, read, and pray every day?

3. Ask God for encouragement in your pursuit of spending time alone with him. Choose today to believe that you can change your life for the better with God's help. Choose to seek first the kingdom of God, acknowledging that your Father will provide for you every good thing as you seek him first.

"But seek first the kingdom of God and his righteousness, and all these things will be added to you" (Matthew 6:33).

GO . . .

There is no failure in your life that can keep you from the promises of God. When God declares his desire to meet with you, there is nothing in the way of you meeting with him. No matter what you choose today, tomorrow, or in the days to come, God is always filled with the desire to spend time alone with you. Allow his passionate pursuit of you to draw you in. Don't worry about tomorrow; simply choose him today. As you choose him moment by moment, he will take you further and deeper than you ever thought possible. May the days of your life be filled with decisions to choose God and marked by the abundant, heavenly fruit of those decisions. And may his presence in your life change, redeem, and empower you to experience and share the remarkable abundance afforded us as God's people, made whole by and in his love.

Where to Go from Here

Congratulations on finishing *Catalyst*! I hope and trust that across these last 28 days you've been drawn even deeper into the reality and goodness of God and that you feel more equipped to have a fresh experience with him every day. God has so much in store for you as you simply make space to meet with him. Every morning, he is knocking on the door of your heart, beckoning you to experience his goodness and center your day around his guidance, presence, and steadfast love. So what's left is for you to find an effective rhythm or tool to open the door of your heart and let in the love and light of God.

To that end, I want to make you aware of a daily devotional my team and I produce called *First15*. We've found that Christians know the importance of a daily quiet time consisting of Bible reading and prayer, yet many struggle with finding a devotional resource that is both easy to understand and relevant to daily life. We've created a devotional for every day of the year comprised of Scripture, guided moments of prayer and reflection, fresh worship, and a call to action. Tens of thousands of readers use *First15* every day to discover God more deeply, and it's changed their lives.

First15 is donor-based, allowing us to offer it to our readers for free. If you've found *Catalyst* helpful, I want to encourage you to sign up to receive *First15* by email. It comes early every morning, giving you a fresh opportunity to spend effective time alone with God in the first 15 minutes of every day.

You can go to **First15.org** to check out *First15* and find additional resources to help you in your pursuit of experiencing God.

May God bless you as you seek him.

1. Charles Duhigg, *The Power of Habit: Why We Do What We Do in Life and Business* (New York: Random House, 2012).

2. Brennan Manning, *Abba's Child: The Cry of the Heart for Intimate Belonging* (Carol Stream: NavPress, 2002).

3. James Finley, *Merton's Palace of Nowhere* (Notre Dame: Ave Maria Press, 2003).

4. Oswald Chambers, *If Ye Shall Ask* (Grand Rapids: Zondervan).